ONE DIRECTION

WHO WE ARE

our autobiography

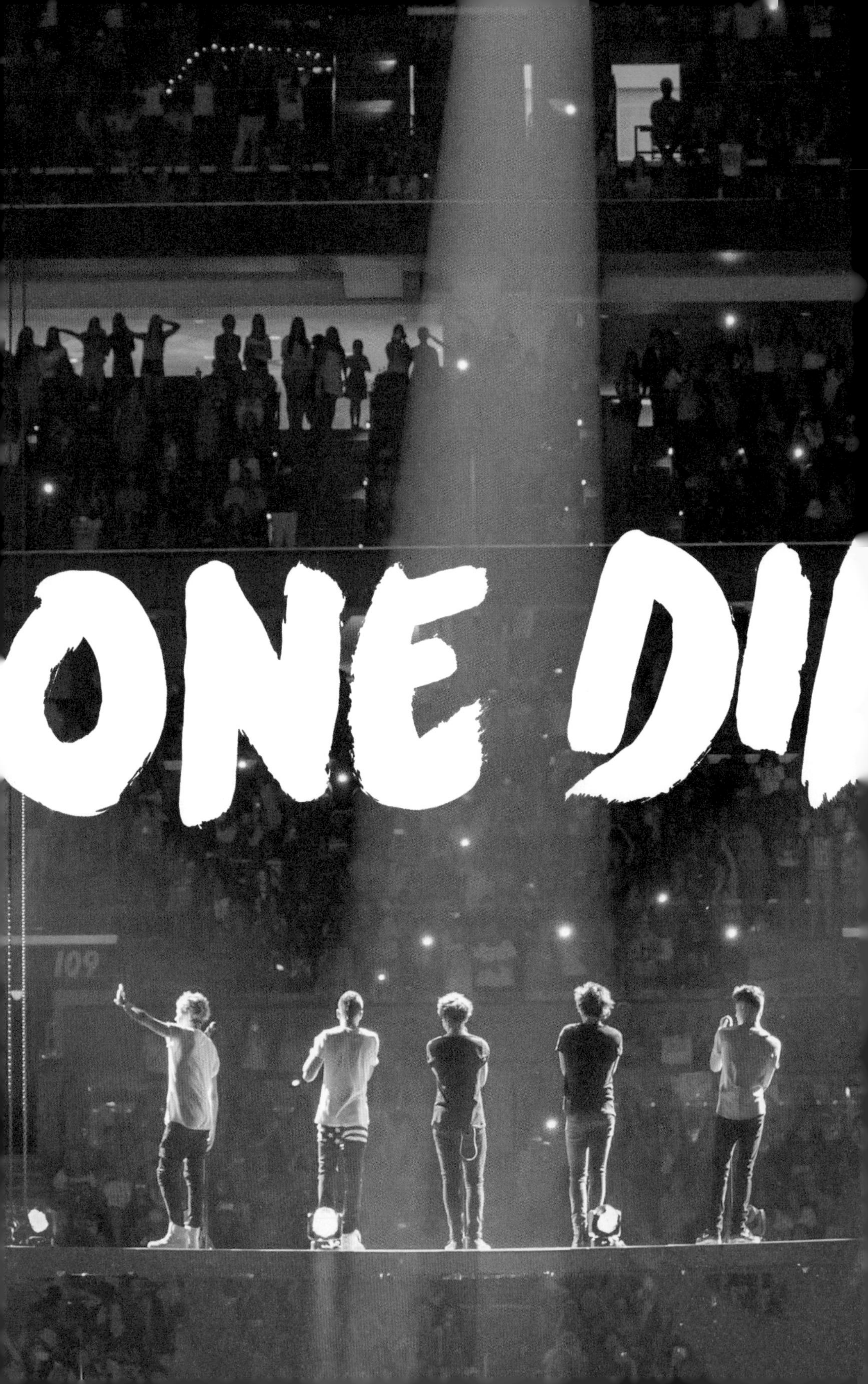
ONE DI
109

RECTION

WHO WE ARE

our autobiography

HarperCollins*Publishers*
77–85 Fulham Palace Road,
Hammersmith, London W6 8JB

www.harpercollins.co.uk

First published by
HarperCollins*Publishers* 2014

10 9 8 7 6 5 4 3 2 1

Design: Martin Topping

One Direction's official photographer is
Calvin Aurand. Calvin Aurand is a music
industry executive turned live music
filmmaker and photographer. For the
past 30 months he has toured with
One Direction, using his unique perspective
and behind-the-scenes access to
document the band's travels around the
globe. For more information visit www.krop.
com/calvinaurand.

All photographs © Calvin Aurand, with the
exception of childhood images and
Instagram images courtesy of Modest!
Management and One Direction;
and texture backgrounds and borders
© shutterstock.com.

A catalogue record of this book is available
from the British Library

HB ISBN 978-0-00-757731-6
PB ISBN 978-0-00-757732-3
EB ISBN 978-0-00-757733-0

Recording our third album, shooting the film
and then writing this book, among many
other things, have just reminded us all how
much our fans have done for us . . . and still
do to this day. We put the finishing touches
to this book as we started travelling around
the world for our stadium tour in 2014, and
performing in front of you every night meant
we were able to say thank you in person to
lots of you guys. But we'd also like to say it
again here – our fans are the greatest in the
world. No one can argue with that! All five
of us know how fortunate we are to have
you supporting us. Thank you from the
bottom of our hearts for everything you've
done for us.

thank you!

We'd also like to thank our family and
friends for being there every step of the
way, and also to mention the following
people for helping us create this book:
Natalie Jerome, Emily Barrett, Rachel Kenny,
Martin Topping, James Empringham,
Monica Green, Alan Cracknell, Simon Gerratt
and everyone at HarperCollins; Simon,
Sonny and all at Syco; the team at Modest!,
including Richard, Harry, Will, Marco, Kim,
Katie, Sheema and Jane; Roma Martyniuk
and Matt Irwin. And a very special thank
you to Martin Roach for helping us tell our
story.

Colour reproduction by FMG
Printed and bound in China by
South China Printing Co. Ltd.

Liam 16

Niall 82

Harry 146

Zayn 212

Louis 272

the boys 334

So much happens to One Direction all the time that we barely get a chance to catch our breath. It's been like that since the *X Factor* days and it's still like that now. Everything goes so fast it can be hard to comprehend or take it all in. Even now, as we write this book and play the first shows of our stadium world tour, it's still difficult to register everything that's taken place. Writing this book has given us all a chance to press 'pause' for a moment, to reflect on what's happened, to look back and really enjoy it all. And because so much goes on all the time, there seems to be so much we want to talk about.

There are quite a few consequences of the fact that, from day one, our fans have been absolutely instrumental in our success. We all know that without you guys on social media, things might have been very different for this band. Another key consequence is that all of our fans know pretty much every detail of our lives, what we're doing on a particular day, who we're hanging out with, where we're recording or travelling to, all that stuff, instantly. You also know our back story. Previous books, thousands of magazine and radio interviews, TV shows, documentaries – even our own film – have told you the tale. There's so much that you already know about us. You already know our dates of birth, how many siblings we have, where we recorded, who with, when we toured, all our charts positions – all the specific details of being in One Direction. So in one sense it's quite a challenge to write a book that you'll find revealing or an eye-opener.

Because of all this we have not used this book to list every award, every gig, every chart position and statistic in our career. There's no point doing that. Instead, what we've tried to do is explain how we *feel*. We want you to get an insight into what our emotions and thoughts were at various stages along the way. To expand a little on how this journey has felt for us five lads, from inside the crazy world of One Direction. Liam often hears about band news and goes, 'How mad is that?!' That's his genuine reaction. Well, hopefully this book will tell you a little more about how we all react to the events that make up life in One Direction.

We've also tried to be honest with our feelings, so when we've had a difficult time we've said exactly that. Fortunately One Direction are a band that has enjoyed a large amount of success, but this doesn't mean that there aren't times when one of us might be struggling a little. That's particularly true on tour when we're thousands of miles from home and maybe weeks away from being able to go back to our fantastically supportive family and friends. That can be hard – it would be ridiculous to pretend otherwise. One Direction are not some perfect pop bubble. We do argue sometimes. Things don't always go to plan. However, being in One Direction has brought so many positives to all of our lives, and we can only feel fortunate and grateful for the opportunities this band has given us.

We started the band with a very naïve and essentially inno-cent view of the music business – and also of life in general. We make no apologies for that. We were just a bunch of kids who thought it would be a good idea to stand in a queue for a famous TV show and see where it took each of us. Looking back, that naïvety actually fuelled us through the completely mad first few months of this band. We were just throwing ourselves at whatever was put in front of us next and we had

Introduction

an energy that seemed to be well received and popular. As the youngest member of One Direction, Harry openly talks about this naïvety and it's something we can all now look back on and see ourselves.

Obviously, a few years down the line, we've all become more experienced with our jobs, but we've also matured and grown up as individuals. So we can't say we're exactly the same people as those starry-eyed kids who got that break on TV back in 2010. However, the thousands of miles flying across the globe, the hundreds of TV shows and gigs, and the thousands of interviews and photo shoots should never be allowed to change who you are as a person. It sounds like a typical pop cliché, but it's true. We're still the same. Older, wiser, and yes, we now have a few life lessons under our belts too, but we're the same. At least, that's how we feel.

We're under an intense spotlight and that's certainly not a problem for any of us, but we've tried to explain how that can feel. At times it's a little uncomfortable, at other times it can provide the maddest and most insanely brilliant moments. Niall explains inside how he thinks he's one of the worst celebrities in the world, and we all feel that way, pretty much. Obviously One Direction are a band with a fairly high profile, and we've been lucky enough to sell a good amount of records and tickets and all that. But that doesn't make us celebrities, whatever that word means anyway. It certainly doesn't make us any different to anyone else in the street. Yes, we might be recognised if we go out and about, but that's just a superficial and unavoidable part of what we do. None of us wants to be called celebrities. Why would you want that?

We try to maintain as close a relationship with our fans as possible. It can sometimes be harder than it used to be, but we're all very conscious of the huge role you fans have played in this band becoming as successful as it is. You can see from this book that there's one overwhelming emotion that repeatedly catches us out – amazement at what you, the fans, do for us day after day after day. It's easy for people to be cynical and say that we don't mean that, to snipe that we've lived inside a bubble these last few years and we can't actually be in touch with our fans. But in our opinion that's just wrong.

Even though the band has progressed from those five naïve lads who made it to the last three of *The X Factor* to playing stadiums all around the world, we're still constantly amazed by the support we get from the fans. It shows itself in all sorts of ways that we find hard to compute – the albums doing so well, breaking records, thousands of people turning up to events like book signings or the *Today* show in New York, or just to an airport or hotel where we happen to be, and our own movie being a big success. The list of the ways in which you fans have backed us all the way seems endless.

The ultimate culmination of all of you championing One Direction is selling out our stadium tour. That tour is, clearly, the biggest series of shows we've ever done. Some of the venues – in fact all of them! – are just massive. Yet, at the time of writing, even after playing a few of the early shows down in South America, we've all noticed that the intimacy that we have with our fans is still there. Once you lose that intimacy, any band is in trouble. To us, it still feels like we're all just meeting up for a great night out.

We've always gigged hard and we enjoy playing live so much. That's the case whether it's our own tours or a one-off like the Olympics. You'll also see in this book that we still find it amazing that so many people come out to see our own shows. Zayn says it blows his mind when he sees so many faces, and he tries to think of all the individual train or car journeys, the time off work, the effort, the energy that has been involved in getting to the show. That pretty much sums up how we all feel. Just because we are in a band that sells a lot of records doesn't mean we don't care about our fans and what they're thinking, doing and feeling.

That's also why the release of *Midnight Memories* meant so much to us and why it was so important that you fans enjoyed that record – because we'd been so heavily involved in the songwriting, because we'd poured a lot of our thoughts and feelings into it, we really wanted you to lock into that, to 'get' that record. It was proof that we still have that closeness with our fans. Great songs are such an important part of this band. In fact, rather than grow more distant from One Direction as each year goes by, we've all found that our desire to write songs and be more and more creatively involved with the music has pulled us into the band even further.

Obviously exhilaration and excitement are a pretty constant feature of our story. We're not gonna pretend that One Direction hasn't been just the most incredibly exciting time of our lives. But there's also a whole other bunch of feelings we've experienced, such as surprise, a lack of confidence, bafflement, homesickness, sadness, nervousness, being starstruck, nerve-wracking uncertainty . . . we've been through so much together! Some nights your head hits the pillow and it's just so hard to process everything that's going on. As Louis repeatedly says in his chapter, the best way he's found to deal with that has been to just 'keep on keeping on', try not to over-analyse things and just enjoy the ride. And what a ride it's been!

When this book's published, it will still be less than four years since we all auditioned for *The X Factor*. Some bands take that long between albums. Most kids spend longer than that at secondary school. So in many ways it isn't a very long period of time. Yet in other ways those auditions are a lifetime away. Maybe because so much is compressed into each One Direction day, it means we feel like we've lived a whole life in just those few short years. Three albums, two world tours, a million memories. Hopefully, this book will give you a glimpse of what we were thinking and feeling as that life happened to us and, of course, your own role in that amazing story.

This is who we are.

WE'VE SAID IT A MILLION TIMES BEFORE, BUT GENUINELY...

THANK YOU.

HARRY,
LIAM,
LOUIS,
NIALL,
ZAYN
XXX

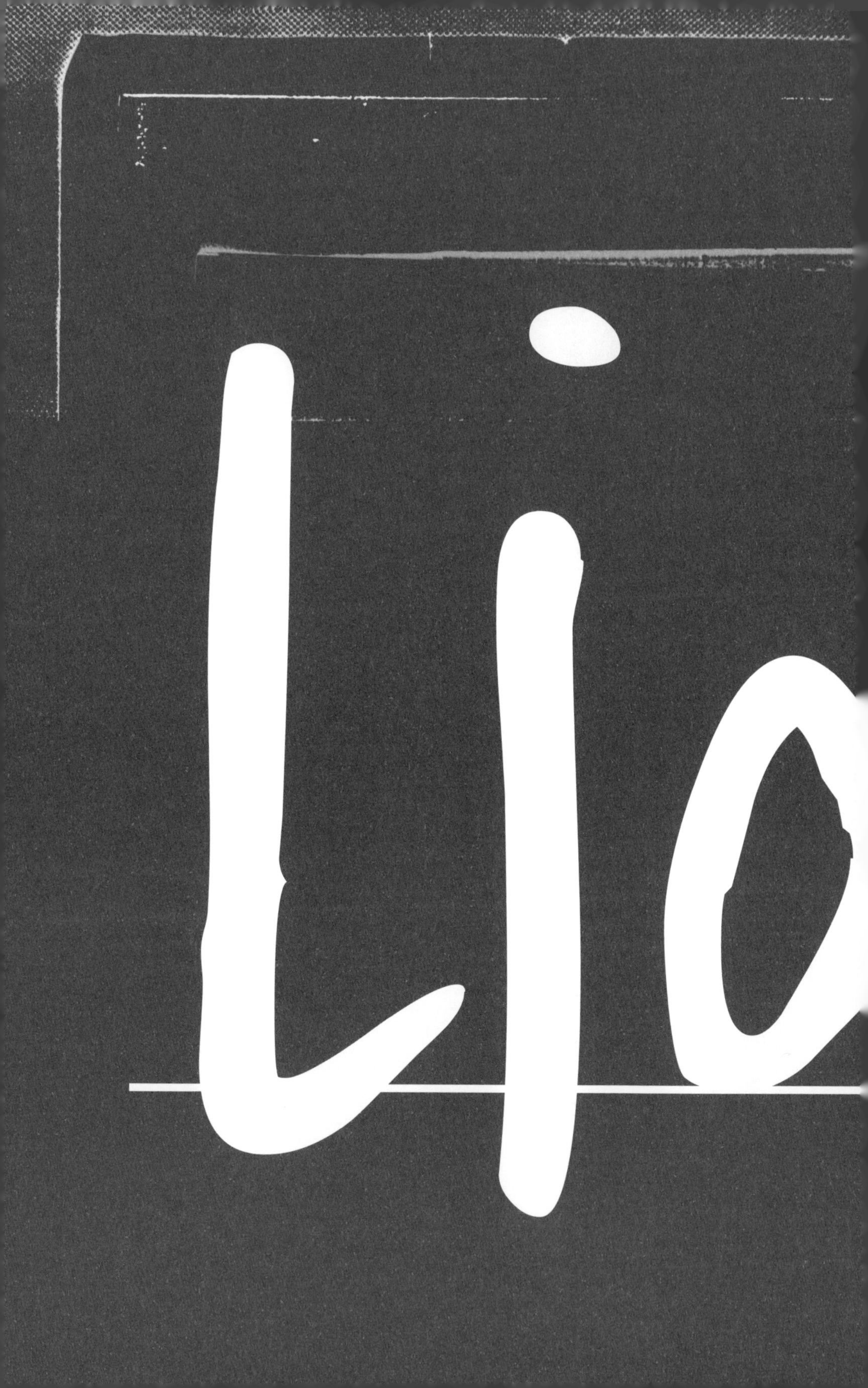
Lio

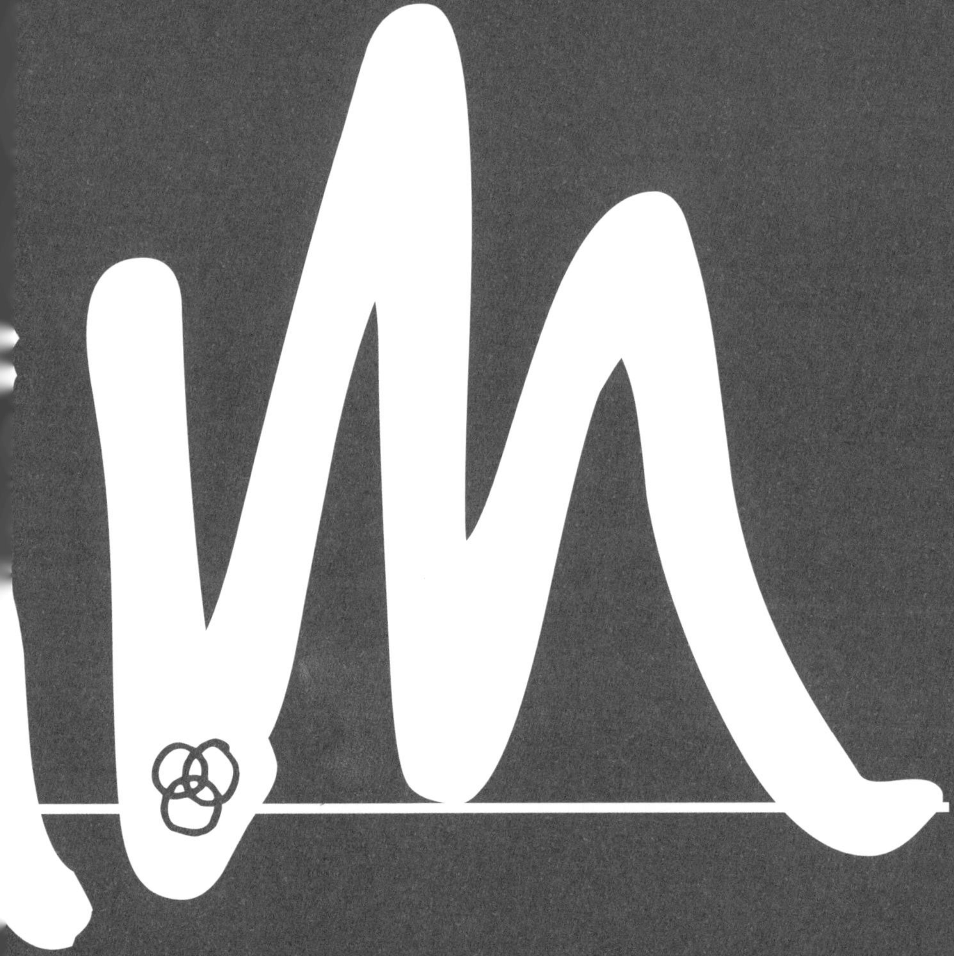

It's hard to believe that I was only 17 when One Direction started. That feels like a different lifetime to me now – so much has happened since this band began. Inevitably, because we've been quite successful, when I look back at my life it's coloured by the whole One Direction experience.

I see traits in my personality now that I know help me in the band, but when I think about it I can see them in me as a kid too. I was always on the go as a young lad – I needed to be doing something all the time. I used to be everywhere, all over the place, especially when I was in my early teens. It used to annoy my dad 'cos I'd want to go and play football over the field by my house or go running. I'd come home completely covered in mud after playing football all day and Dad would say, 'You smell like a sweaty little boy!' He always used to say that. Eventually I had a pair of trousers for every day of the week 'cos it was impossible for my mum to keep up with the washing. 'Liam! You're always so busy, busy, busy! You never sit still! Where do you get the energy from?' Busy, busy, busy. I was sitting in half my classes covered in mud and after school my parents would rip me to bits: 'What do you think you're doing walking round like that? Do you know who that reflects on?!' I was only having a bit of fun ... I just found it hard to sit still. Boxing and athletics were good outlets for all that energy. I loved my sports, still do.

I used to bounce off the walls at home a fair bit too. We lived in a three-bedroom house with five people – Mum, Dad and my sisters Ruth and Nicola. We were a tight family and we loved each other, of course, but the house was small and crammed with all our stuff in it so there were times when we'd argue. Mum and Dad were always having to be careful with money and work hard, and we sometimes did get on top of one another. It's inevitable, I suppose. There were just too many kids growing up in a small house. I'd want to watch my favourite show on the telly but my sisters would want to see their stuff, or we'd be arguing over something and nothing. I'd shout into the kitchen, 'Mum, I want to watch the football but Ruth says she's watching something else!' but Mum was just trying to get everything sorted around the house and

When I was a kid I was constantly running, playing football, messing about outside – on the go all the time – so I spent a lot of time in the shower later!

keep everyone happy! Typical family stuff, really, but because the house was so small we were in each other's faces the whole time.

So I used to spend a lot of time outside, playing football, going over the field and causing a bit of trouble, just playing with my mates. Then as soon as I got home I'd be up into my bedroom on the PlayStation. I guess I was quite independent at times. I suppose all teenagers have that phase, to be fair.

However, one thing that I always absolutely loved doing was singing. Choirs, a local performing-arts group . . . karaoke when I was a little older. Wherever and whenever I could sing or perform, I would. My dad was amazing. When I was a kid he was my driving force to get out there and perform to people. I never saw anything like this – as in One Direction – happening. In fact I don't think anybody could ever have seen this coming. But for some reason – whether he was just crazy or not, I don't know – Dad was convinced I'd end up doing something in music. 'Liam,' he'd say, 'you've just got to get out there and perform. We need to get you more and more gigs. You can sing, and you've got what it takes, son. You can do this, I know you can.' He thought that I'd maybe do just a solo record in the UK, but never anything world-wide. Then One Direction kicked off. So maybe he wasn't the crazy one after all?

Back in the day he used to take me to all my gigs, he cut my CDs for me to put my backing tracks on, he'd do my sound, all the driving. He was like my tour manager when I was young, and if I did something wrong I'd get a telling off from him the same way as I would now from One Direction's tour manager, Paul. Dad taught me so much.

22

That impulse to always be busy carried over into my singing. As a kid I was constantly after doing more and more gigs. I didn't care where they were or who I was singing to – I just wanted to perform, graft and learn. Dad would say, 'Liam, I've got you a gig in this local club, but it's pretty small and there's no money in it', and I'd be like, 'I don't care, Dad, let's do it. Bring it on.' We were both like that, to be fair. No gig was too small or too far away. Whatever, whenever, we both knew any shows at this point were all great experience for me. This has served me well in One Direction because it's meant that when the madness all kicked off I was at least reasonably experienced already. That's why I used to start all the band songs off back then, because the management knew I'd been on stage many times before. We were so young when One Direction started and I guess it made sense to utilise whatever limited experience we did have.

I'm proud that I did a lot of groundwork for the band when I was younger. I performed to some of the strangest crowds you could ever play to! I once played in Rhyl at this event called the Sunshine Festival. Except it was tipping down with rain and I don't remember seeing any sunshine the whole day. It was decent money (£50 for three songs, I seem to remember), but when I got up on stage there were about ten people – maximum! – just standing around in a field looking bored. I still made the effort, though, 'Hello Rhyl!' I was jumping all over the stage, and I remember there was this one mother feeding her baby with a spoon the whole time while I bounced around like a nutter. That was an odd gig.

On another occasion I played the Oceana Centre in Wolverhampton, which was near where I lived. The crowd was a

I have very fond memories of family holidays as a kid, I was always up to something, never sitting still, great fun!

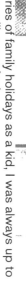

bit lively and about halfway through the second song this lad just dashed a 50p coin at me. It hit my face, cutting my cheek open. I had two songs left and no way was I gonna let him stop me, so I dabbed the blood off, carried on and finished the set. 'Thanks, mate!'

It wasn't all baby food and coin-throwing, of course. I used to get paid quite well sometimes. I remember getting £350 for six minutes' work at one show, which for a 14-year-old lad felt pretty amazing! And, of course, as a lot of people know, I was lucky enough to sing 'Black & Gold' at Wolverhampton Wanderers' stadium one time. They can fit nearly 30,000 people in that bad boy and, because it was before their game against Man Utd, the ground was rammed. I was really nervous but I got a great round of applause, which was a relief because I wasn't sure how a football crowd would react to some kid coming out and singing. Mind you, I didn't tell them I was a Baggies fan!

By the time I entered *The X Factor* the first time, aged 14, I really fancied performing as a career. My dad had always said, 'I want Simon Cowell to hear your voice, Liam. We just need to get you in front of Simon ...' So when they dropped the age restriction to 14, I was on that website filling in the form quick as a flash. It all looks pretty manageable on the telly in a way, but actually you need guts to have a pop at *The X Factor*. I was only a kid, so it was a huge step to try to get in the competition, queue for hours and hours, then actually set foot on the stage when you know you're about to sing for Simon and the judges. And then the day itself – getting up early, making my slot, keeping the nerves under control and not crumbling – that was all a big ask. I just kept

Top: I was a very keen amateur runner in my childhood and had ambitions to represent England.
Middle: My hopes of becoming Wolverhampton's first ever quad bike world champion were destined to fail.
Bottom: Singing was a constant in my life from an early age. I loved performing as often as I possibly could – still do!

Liam

Top: With one of several running trophies I managed to win as a junior.
Bottom: At the O2 for Boot Camp the first time I tried out for *The X Factor*.

reminding myself how much I enjoyed singing and harnessed the feeling that I wanted to show the judges what I could do.

It was gutting to lose out at Judges' Houses, of course, but I tried to console myself with the fact that I'd got to the last 24 out of 118,000. Plus Simon had said I was talented, which was hugely encouraging. The whole experience was pretty intense for a 14-year-old, and I actually think that if I'd done well as a solo singer in that first *X Factor*, I'm not sure how it would have panned out for me afterwards. I certainly can't see how it would have competed with One Direction. I was still gutted at the time, of course. But after I'd licked my wounds, the experience focused my mind on just how much I wanted to make a go of my singing. 'Come on, Dad, let's book some more gigs. I want to get back out there again straight away . . .'

After that, me and Dad took it really seriously. We upped the number of gigs I was playing, tried to get the word out there and started making a few contacts in the industry. I even started to write a few songs, although I'm not sure they'll make it onto the new One Direction album! I can actually remember the very first song I ever wrote – it was kinda like a *Spiderman* soundtrack. I still have it on my laptop and it's not a bad song, to be fair. I went to a recording studio that was literally just this geezer's house and we did the recording in the back room. That doesn't sound very glamorous but, with a lot of One Direction's songs being written on the road, it's not so very different to how we end up recording much of the band's music!

We made a few inroads with people who appeared to be well positioned to help, but we just seemed to keep coming

Liam

We're
back
for you
tomorrow, LA!

193k 338k 140

LIAM

to dead-ends and things falling through at the last minute. I was gigging pretty constantly and writing a few songs with people who took them to record labels ... but nothing happened. One geezer I was working with just upped and went off to Hawaii, so that all fell apart. I went to so many gigs that turned out to be disappointments. I did that first solo shot at *The X Factor*, which stalled at Judges' Houses. And then, as you know, two years later I went to *The X Factor* again ... and, once again, it didn't go well and I was rejected as a solo artist.

Only this time it wasn't over, was it?

The entire *X Factor* experience was obviously a pivotal moment in my life and I honestly look back on it with only great memories. Yes, it was hard work and it was certainly very nerve-wracking on occasions, but how can you reflect on that experience and see anything other than fantastic times? And what an opportunity it gave us five lads.

We've all spoken about being on *The X Factor* so many times but to be frank it now feels like a world away. It feels so, so long ago. When we were on the show, we were just concentrating on enjoying ourselves and having a good time. There were a lot of contestants who were very serious about the competition, which is fair enough, and there was a little bit of cattiness backstage ... but we were chillin' and we were friends with everyone, more or less. You all already know about my dreadful disappointment at being rejected and then the intense, overwhelming excitement of being put into a band with these four other lads, but even to this day that moment when they revealed they were putting us into

One Direction is still just the most amazing memory. Hard to believe, really!

Back then we used to offend so many people with our, I guess what you'd call, vulgar language. But we didn't see that – we were just kids having a good time. We'd be sat doing some interview – or just backstage or out and about somewhere – and the jokes would start escalating, then eventually one of us would cross a line and I'd be like, 'I can't believe you said that!', but I'd be laughing my head off at the same time. Our level of professionalism was horrible. When we first came off the show, the very next day we had to go straight into Syco for a telling off! It was about something we'd said that was just funny – I can't repeat what it was. We were like, 'We didn't mean any harm!' We were just typical teenage lads who liked to go out, have a good time and mess about! At this point I was really sensible compared with the other lads, proper shy, really, and I used to keep the banter levels down a bit. I'd be like, 'I think we've overstepped the mark there, lads!' or I'd tell them if I thought they'd been too vulgar. That's why I got the nickname of 'Daddy Direction'.

Now we're a few albums in we'd like to think we know a little bit about the music industry, but back then, jeez, we knew absolutely nothing! It's bizarre to think that we were thrown in so deep, so quickly. Even basic things like moving to London were a massive deal. 'Hey, Mum, I'm coming home for a bit 'cos I'm moving to London next week and I need to pack everything' – it was literally that mad. I was 17 years old at the time and had to move out of my parents' house to this huge city, somewhere I'd only been a couple of times with my dad for recording. So it was pretty scary, 'cos I didn't really know what to expect from the capital. When I was a kid my dad used to say to me, 'Liam, if you get through on *X Factor*, don't come back until Christmas.'

Well, I haven't moved back since.

Those first few months of One Direction were just a blur. It was madness, really weird, but we went with it and loved every second. When you're that young and inexperienced, you don't really know what the heck is going on. People are like, 'This is where you're going to live, we'll pay for this, we'll do this for you but you have to pay for that, then you need to go into work on that day . . .' It all moves so fast, it's insane.

You really don't know what's happening. *The X Factor* is more or less like watching a band with a development deal but right in front of the nation every week. That was One Direction. We started off in full public view and it's never really changed since.

We were going into interviews and saying all sorts of stuff, just honest, funny, straight answers. Luckily, the newspapers were really good to us. They didn't take advantage of our inexperience and really helped us along in those early days. We were so terrible it was awful! We were just kids, so naïve, who'd literally been dropped into this massive industry that will eat you alive if you do it wrong. And we were doing everything wrong! Yet somehow it seemed to work. People wanted to talk to us, find out about our music, get to know us. Something was going on . . . we must have had some sort of Guardian Angel.

In some sense, that Guardian Angel was our fans. Even before we'd signed a record deal, social media around the

band was going nuts. We all had various accounts before the band was formed, but it quickly became apparent after the show that something was going on out there. I'm deeply appreciative of that fanbase working so hard on social media – it's such a huge deal for us and a massive part of our story. I personally think it started when people saw us on *X Factor* YouTube videos and there was '#OneDirection' posted, which started being one of the top ten trending topics in the UK most weeks. People began re-tweeting and we were just watching this start to blow up right before our eyes. There was an army of fans out there promoting and championing the band. We were all like, 'This is crazy! How brilliant is that?'

Right from the word go we gigged hard too. When we started off playing those very early shows it was going OK, but management have always been nervous about when we go on stage, because we're just too laid back about things. There'd be some really important show or appearance and they'd (quite rightly) say stuff like, 'This is a big gig, a real opportunity to showcase the band, OK?' and we'd be like, 'Yeah, great, let's have a crack at it!' We were rough around the edges at times, but there were some great gigs back then and we were just having an amazing time giving it a go. We started in Scotland, doing a couple of gigs on the club circuit up there. The first gig was really good. I remember very clearly being on a small stage in this very hot room full of about 300 people. Even before we started singing the security were dragging girls out of the audience because they were fainting. I remember thinking, *That's a bit odd.* We were on stage trying to be all happy, and I could see girls crying and screaming 'cos they were getting crushed. It was baffling, to be honest.

One of the next gigs was in Leeds and there happened to be a lot of lads in the club that night. There were all these girls' screams that went on for a certain length of time and then you'd hear these boos underneath. I kept winking at this one girl, and then I realised she was there with her boyfriend and he was getting proper riled up! We played all over the place, even in places like G.A.Y., which we clearly weren't old enough to go to ourselves. However, we all felt this was our groundwork, as it were, and we knew it was important to put the miles in. I was just drawing on my experience of gigs from before the band, and kept saying to the lads, 'These gigs are like our apprenticeship and this is how we prove ourselves as a band. We've had the most amazing headstart, but this is when it is really going to count.' The amount of promo and PAs, the *X Factor* tour, hundreds of photo-shoots – the workload was massive. At the same time there was also a huge element of luck: right place, right time, with the right technology available to make it happen, to introduce One Direction to the rest of the world.

Of course, it wasn't all luck and people being friendly to us. Our record label did a great job at the start, finding us brilliant talent to write the songs for us. That soon became apparent when we started recording sessions for the début album. When we were recording 'What Makes You Beautiful' at our first studio session in Sweden, we'd tweeted some studio bits and pieces and these two girls came down on a train from miles away to where we were in Stockholm. We hadn't even got a record out at that point. Once the fanbase had music to go along with all this social media interest as well, it just kicked off big time.

The first album sessions themselves were interesting! Flying to LA and Sweden was very exciting, of course, particularly the West Coast of America, which to us five seemed like such a glamorous location. Flash hotels, big recording studios, famous producers – it was all so much to take in. To be really honest, there was a bit of 'discussion', shall we say, with the label about the song choices. They wanted different things to what we initially wanted, but in the end it did go the right way, the way that it should have done.

We kinda got told how to sing a little bit on that album, as the people we were working with had a very particular way of doing things. We're much more loose about it now, but they were very exact about our pronunciation, getting all the 'S's and the 'T's correct. I'd sing a line that was bang in tune and sounded great, and the producers would say, 'Can you do that again, please? We just need a little more clarity on the last word, it has to be perfect …' It was all very intricate and precise. And let's face it, what they did worked. There was a learning curve for us five in the band, but we were learning off top industry people. We got on well with everyone in the studio and built up friendships with them, but we were so naïve to that environment; it kinda felt like we were still on *The X Factor* so we just went with it like that.

By the time our début single 'What Makes You Beautiful' came out in September 2011 there was intense interest in the band. So that first release was a huge moment for us. The song had to do well and I don't mind admitting I was a bit nervous about it. I said to the one of the lads, I think it was

Louis, 'I don't like the drum roll before the chorus kicks in …
I'm not sure about that,' but the producers knew exactly
what they were doing, because sure enough it was a massive
song, amazing for us. Being Number 1 was an incredible
feeling, but there was no time to reflect on that achievement
as we were just straight on to the next thing. Once that was
out and had done well, the momentum just kept mounting
and mounting.

Our début album *Up All Night* was released at the start
of December and, even with all the massive PR we were
getting, none of us expected the record to do as well as it did:
Number 2 in the UK and topping the charts in 17 countries!
Madness! We were bemused, to be honest. We'd be sitting in
the the tour bus or in a studio and someone would phone us
to say we'd hit Number 1 in yet another country, and we'd be
like, 'Is this for real?' It was the most incredible time.

Again, there was barely a moment's pause before we were
straight on to the next thing, with no chance to soak up the
news. For starters, we had our first headline tour lined up
around UK theatres to support the album. Despite all the
craziness at that point in our careers, we didn't rush anything
in terms of huge gigs: we didn't try to play multiple nights
at the O2 straight away, or say, 'Come on, people have
slept in the street for three days for tickets, why don't we play
Wembley Arena?' We didn't say that. There were a few pretty
big venues on that tour, to be fair, but generally we just
wanted to take our time and progress as naturally as possible. I'd say to the lads, 'Remember what we agreed?
We need to learn our craft, play the smaller stages, work our
way up from the bottom. We have to respect the process.'

the
Signing hAs
Started!!
1DHQ

For example, the second-ever night of One Direction headlining live we sang the entire chorus of 'Gotta Be You' completely out of tune because we didn't really know what we were doing with the wedges or the in-ears. We were all like, 'Oh my God, it was awful!' AWFUL! I dread to think what some of those people in the audience thought. They must have definitely turned their backs on us for ever! We were terrible. We were naïve and didn't really know what was going on – some of us still don't know today! But that was just a phase of us learning, and you've gotta be bad sometimes in order to get good. There's always a learning curve. That said, we were getting such a reaction it was incredible. The venues were quite modest and so the fans were right in our faces. I'd be trying to sing, and the fans would be screaming and shouting, 'Liam! Liam!' so loud it hurt . . . Those were great times.

The spotlight was pretty intense that Christmas, as the tour did well and our album kept hitting Number 1 in various countries. That was weird. Good weird! We were scheduled to head over to the US shortly after the New Year, expectations were positive, and we were all really excited and hoped that maybe a few of the kids out there had heard of us.

We arrived in the States to start our campaign in February 2012, having signed a US record deal the previous autumn. We got a massive break straight away by being offered a slot opening up for Big Time Rush, who at the time had their own TV show and were massive. What we didn't realise was the scale of the reaction we were about to get ourselves! One time we were on our way to an interview and I said to

By the second song of the very first gig it was apparent that they knew **every word of every song!**

Harry, 'Do you think these people will have a clue who we are?' How wide of the mark can you be?

That support tour was proper nuts. Each night we went on stage early doors but we immediately noticed the whole audience was already in the venue. *Strange*. Before the very first Big Time Rush show I'd been worried about going up on stage because I'm the so-called 'hype man' – so I'll stand there and coax everyone to sing the words and join in – but I was just assuming that nobody would know any of our songs, never mind any of the words. How wrong can you be? By the second song of the very first gig it was apparent that they knew every word of every song! I walked across the stage to Zayn and said, 'Is it just me or do these guys know every single lyric?! This is mad!' We also noticed that after we'd finished, loads of fans would leave the venue to come out and meet us. Those shows were amazing. We were just bewildered, really, as no one ever expected that sort of re-action in the States.

The single did pretty well over in the US, but social media was going nuts by now and we were aware that there was a strong interest in the band. Then we were booked to do the *Today* show in New York, which is a really big institution over there. I remember it being absolutely freezing, proper New York cold, and we'd been getting reports on the radio that a lot of people had turned up. I was like, 'Great! How many? A good few hundred, maybe?' Management were obviously getting more detailed figures because they'd be smiling and saying stuff like, 'Er, no, Liam, it's more than a few hundred ...' We just didn't know – this was New York, not London, after all. We walked out on to the street to perform, and when we climbed up on to the stage and saw the full scale of the crowd for the first time it was a big shock. Turned out that 10,000 people had rocked up!

The Rockefeller Plaza stage was on the street in between all these massive skyscrapers. It's a really picturesque location and there were loads of American flags waving around above us, so as you glance around the chaos you suddenly remember you're in the States. It was completely crazy. This was our American national TV début and here we were showing up on a red London bus to play to that many people. Afterwards we found out that we'd broken the record for the show. I'm pretty sure it was held by Lady Gaga, and let's face it she's one of pop's biggest icons, the closest thing we've had to another Madonna for this generation. So for us to be on a similar scale to these sort of people at that stage was just like, 'Good times!'

The album had débuted at Number 1 in multiple countries by then, so all eyes were on how high we could get in the US. With all the hype around the band, the album was brought forward a week – but even then none of us had any idea of what was about to happen. Early on in the week we had a meeting with the record label and management to see how things were going, and they said, 'Look, lads. There's a chance the album could chart very high, but the competition this week is severe and to have any chance of a big chart entry we need to raise our game.' So we did. We took on mountains of extra promo. I remember staying up until stupid o'clock in the morning signing 5,000 CDs while doing a load of press interviews. We left no stone unturned. We put in two extra book signings when we were supposed to be chillin' and having downtime, but we wanted that Number 1 so bad. That would be our calling card: to be able to say our album was Number 1 in the States. We totally worked our arses off that week, going round so many places to make it work.

At the end of the week I was sitting in a yellow New York cab when my phone rang. It was our manager, Will. 'Liam, I've got some news, the album's charted as a new entry straight in at Number 1!' I just couldn't believe what I was hearing. I got straight out of the cab and went and bought myself a new watch to celebrate the occasion! That's a little ritual I have now: every time we do something cool I buy a nice watch to commemorate the achievement. I thought about getting a tattoo each time, but as we've been lucky enough to have so many hits I'd be completely covered by now! If I do have kids when I'm older I'll be able to give the watches to them and explain the story behind each one.

To be totally frank with you, none of us were fully aware of the significance of hitting Number 1 in the US with our début album. I mean, don't get me wrong, we knew it was BIG, but it wasn't until a few weeks later when it had sunk in that we started to realise exactly what it meant. The Beatles had never done it. The Rolling Stones, Take That, Coldplay – all these massive bands had never managed to get their début album to hit Number 1. How crazy is that? That's also a record that can't be broken because it was a first, which I love.

Everything went completely nuts from that moment on. Proper nuts! Whatever we thought was mad before the album came out was just a fraction of how insane it was about to become.

THEN ONE OF THE LADS WOULD SAY SOMETHING, OR DO SOMETHING STUPID AND MAKE ME LAUGH, AND I'D BE FINE AGAIN

We're often asked *why* our album went to Number 1 in the US and why it all went so nuts. I think there are several reasons. For starters, I think it helped that we were just having a great time, and perhaps people enjoyed watching that. Like I said, we didn't know the history behind the *Billboard* charts. Honestly, I didn't really know jack about music when we started. I loved singing and performing, but I just used to do covers and didn't know anything about music history. I do now – I listen to all sorts of music from way back, check out the charts and keep right up to speed with everything. Back then, though, I was so naïve about it all. I wonder if that was a plus for us? In a way, we never took it seriously and people seemed to like that endearing side of us – that we were like, 'Hey, we're just having a laugh! This is great!' People kinda liked the fact we weren't overly serious about it, that we were just having a good time and dressing like normal lads from round the corner.

I also think we had good songs that were really well written and expertly produced. Adele had certainly opened a lot of doors for British acts over there too. The Big Time Rush tour was a lucky break. Plus, we did work stupid hard. We really went for it. Our American marketing team was amazing, and last but not least you cannot discount the huge power of the internet, in particular our amazing fans and what they did for us on social media. That was crucial. But honestly, I don't really know. It just kicked off. What I do know is it went fast and it went BIG.

The rest of 2012 was a mad blur, to be honest.

* * *

We flew back from America in February for the Brit Awards, where we somehow won 'Single of the Year' for our début song. Since then we've luckily won a fair few awards, but awards ceremonies are a bit weird sometimes. I remember the first VMA win – that was a big night and one of my fondest memories of the early days. It felt so important to get that recognition in the States.

The first Brit Awards were a big deal for us too. I've watched those programmes since I was a kid and I've always thought, *I wonder what it's actually like, the moment they say you've won?* The only problem we had that night was that back in the day I was known as the responsible one, so in the dressing room beforehand one of our managers, Richard Griffiths, handed me a blue sheet of paper and said, 'Here are all the people it would be great for you to thank if we win.' So when they opened the envelope and shouted out, 'And the winner is ...' I was like, 'YES!' then I was like, 'Oh crap, the list!' I'd never done a speech before, and when I got up there the sound was bouncing off the walls and I was struggling to hear myself. I slowed my words down to get round this, which didn't really work – so it was just a mess. I got all the names right, though!

It was quite funny because at that first Brits we were kinda jeered a little bit by a lot of British artists because we'd come from *The X Factor* and people were sceptical about us. It was funny seeing that dynamic change at later awards ceremonies over the next few years, and it's nice to have a bit of respect for having worked hard and achieved success as a British band overseas. One award I would like to mention was handed out at the 'Sons & Daughters' award ceremony

Awards ceremonies can be quite odd nights out, but thankfully we've been lucky enough to scoop quite a few gongs at them!

NICK GATFIELD
CHAIRMAN & CEO OF SONY MUSIC

INVITES YOU TO A PARTY
TO CELEBRATE THE 2013 BRIT AWARDS

WEDNESDAY
20TH
FEBRUARY

10:30PM
UNTIL LATE

THE ARTS CLUB
40 DOVER STREET // W1S 4NP

BY INVITATION ONLY // ADMITS ONE // RSVP

SONY MUSIC   THE ARTS CLUB

in my hometown of Wolverhampton in late 2013. The ceremony recognised local people who the judges felt had made a mark for the city around the world in various ways, so I was absolutely over the moon when I was nominated and then subsequently won an award. Unfortunately I couldn't be there because we were touring Down Under, but Mum and Dad went to pick up the award for me. I did a video message and was just so incredibly proud: 'My band has picked up a lot of awards over the past few years, but for me this is the one I'm definitely most grateful for. Wolverhampton's my home and it always will be. I want to say a massive thank you to all those people years ago who gave me the opportunities I needed to get me where I am today ... It's definitely the most important award. It's going to take pride of place on my shelf.'

During the Big Time Rush tour it had become apparent that our band was bigger than the venues we were playing. Then, with the album's success and all the media interest, the demand for live shows became enormous. So in April we started our own headline tour of Australia and then North America. There was a big buzz around us at the time, and even though there was a lot of pressure in those early days it just seemed to flow together into one mad time. We almost forgot where we were sometimes as it all didn't seem very real. Luckily, we didn't have any bad audiences – everywhere we went we got a great reaction. It was absolutely amazing to be touring round North America for our own shows and we were loving being on the road. It was just us and our tour manager Paul, mostly, crammed into this shady bus that seemed to be stuck together with bits of tape. The shows

kept selling out and the tour kept getting extended, so we eventually ended up doing over 60 shows. Interspersed in among all this was more TV, such as *iCarly* and *Saturday Night Live*, and the madness just kept ramping up and up and up.

The chemistry of the band was still evolving and that tour really helped. Remember, although I'd roomed with Niall on *The X Factor*, we didn't know each other at all when the band first started. We'd had a week at Harry's step-dad's bungalow gaming, watching TV, swimming and just messing about, really, but even on this tour it was still relatively early days in our friendships.

We were still finding our feet in the industry too, so it wasn't always plain sailing. We used to find that before shows everybody around us would be nervous. Management and the crew would sometimes say, 'Are you OK, guys? Everything all right for tonight?' You know, they were just being protective and making sure we were OK. But we were often the most relaxed of all, us five lads. We'd be like, 'We're just here to have a good time!' I think that's more or less what got us through and stopped us crumbling from thinking too much about it. We just carried on with our jobs – we had work to do. If we had forced ourselves to sit down and analyse every bit of success – 'Why are we Number 1 in America? How have we sold this many tickets? Why do the fans overseas like us so much?' – all that stuff, we'd most probably have caved in. Having a laugh was, in retrospect, a really good coping mechanism for processing the most bizarre events going on around us . . . but at the time it wasn't that calculated, it was just what we were doing naturally. The

Special delivery just arrived!

TO BE GIVEN UP

Table No: **14**   Seat: **8**

63229413900242

EON2002 19-52511 X2 B-Arena BRT

security IED · security IED · security IED · security IED · security IED · security IED · security IED · security IED · security IED · security IED · security IED

Entrance: **B**

Table No: **14**   Seat: **8**

Guest:

EON2002 19-52511 X2 B-Arena BRT

BRIT AWARDS 2013 with MasterCard

ARENA FLOOR

Wed 20 Feb • The O2, Peninsula Square, London, SE10 0DX
Doors & Reception 5.00pm • Dinner 5.30pm • Seated 7.45pm
Live Broadcast 8.00pm • Party 10.00pm - 1.00am

BPI
The British Recorded Music Industry

THE BRIT TRUST
Supporting young people in music and education

63229413900242

fact that it helped us relieve the pressure was just an added bonus. We had a right laugh, carrying on having fun with it, not really thinking about all these records and statistics we were being told about. We never really dwelled on these until after we'd finished. Then we were like, 'Blimey, lads, it looks like we smashed it out there!'

2012 was a massive year for the UK because of the London Olympics, which we were absolutely honoured to be invited to perform at. That was a *huge* deal for all of us. As a child athlete, I'd often said to my dad, 'I'll make the Olympics!' – and now I finally had! The line-up of artists involved was amazing and we met a lot of them before the closing ceremony, people like Madness, the Spice Girls and Russell Brand. We performed on the back of this truck, but I didn't care where we sang from, it was such an honour to represent our country around the world. It felt like being called up for an England game – the England game of pop stars. It was huge! The Games were such a hugely proud moment for me to do something so prestigious.

One interviewer asked me, 'Now that you've enjoyed so much success, have you started to re-set your goals? Are you all looking for new ambitions?' but to be perfectly honest the answer is no. We were still kinda just going along with it, having a laugh, taking each day as it came and working as hard as we could. I honestly think a lot of the time things seemed to fall into our laps. I would sometimes say to people, 'We didn't aim to play the Olympics, we just got asked,' or 'We didn't dream we'd play to thousands of people in a street in New York, it just happened.' Obviously, our team in

Liam

thank you for all your support so far!!!

the US and all round the world worked amazingly hard, and they had plans and strategies, of course, I'd never deny that. But in terms of us five lads, we were just riding that wave and it was the best time.

The rest of 2012 was just mad. We released some more singles and won some MTV awards, and all the time we were doing promo and gigs – it was pretty relentless. In the first half of the year we also started working on the second album, and this time we got a bit more involved with the writing. We were aware we'd set a huge benchmark with the previous album, so there was definitely a lot of pressure on us to match what had happened with *Up All Night*, plus we wanted to develop the music to make it better. That said, the album was still essentially in the record label's hands, plus the people writing the songs. We had a certain amount of say in where we wanted to take it but we were certainly not the chief song-writers. Luckily, the songs came in great and I remember feeling very good about the new record at the time. We didn't record much of the material on the road, and there was still quite a bit of conventional studio time in Sweden and London. It was a little bit easier, although there were still a lot of interviews and promo to be done, and there was always something going on while we were recording.

If we thought it was mad with the first album, the second record, *Take Me Home*, just took things on to a whole new level. 'Live While We're Young' had been the lead single, and that had done well, so we knew there was still a lot of interest. I did feel pressure to make a good follow-up but that just made us work even harder. Even so, when we heard the chart news in the first week of release we were all shocked.

The new album hit Number 1 in 31 countries – it was just madness! It's always amazing to get Number 1 in the UK – and we did the same again in the States, another world record. Everywhere we went now it was a frenzy, just sheer chaos. I kept thinking about the album tour and I just couldn't wait to get out there to see all the fans that had made this possible. I still find it incredible that we have so many fans in so many countries – the global scale of what has happened is quite hard to take in, to be honest. In our interviews, one of the most repeated sentences I say must be: 'I can't believe the reception we've got in this country.' It genuinely never ceases to amaze me.

The month after the second album came out we played what is perhaps our most iconic gig to date, at New York's Madison Square Garden. When we'd been working so hard during the week of our début album's release, Steve Barnett from our label Columbia (a Wolves fan!) had said, 'If you get Number 1 with this album then you're going to play Madison Square Garden!' He just put it like that. I was like, 'Woah! Don't be daft, Steve!' But then we did get Number 1 and, sure enough, true to his word, Steve booked us to play MSG. I was properly worried, saying to the other lads, 'Do you think we might have overstepped the mark? It's such a huge and legendary venue ...' I thought we might have over-reached ourselves too early. So imagine how it felt when someone from the record label phoned us and said, 'Lads, the MSG has sold out in less than one minute.' That's 20,000+ tickets. It seemed ludicrous. We were just these young guns off the street ... yet we'd sold out the Garden in a heartbeat. These things just don't happen. That venue is such a prestigious

building, and it wrapped up 2012 so perfectly because after the show we had this big party with all our friends, family and everyone involved in One Direction together to celebrate what had been a ridiculous 12 months.

The X Factor was such a bubble and then with One Direction going so massive so quickly it was in many ways another bubble of mad events and crazy schedules. I can see how easy it would be for someone to kinda lose perspective. Well, in February 2013 we got involved with Comic Relief and a trip to Ghana, and if ever there was a leveller, this was it.

To say it was quite an eye-opener is the understatement of the century. These were two *very* important days for me personally. We did have a nice hotel to stay in, there's no lie about that. I'm not gonna pretend we roughed it, because we didn't. There's a big rich–poor divide in Ghana, so it's not like there are no posh hotels. However, the poverty is just appalling. It was only a two-day trip but we spent 15 hours in a slum, which was easily enough for us to get a picture of that life. Can you imagine living there the whole time?

On one side of this slum was a rubbish tip and on the other side were all these little shacks, literally just 50 yards away from the mountain of rubbish. The smell was horrific, and the wind was blowing that stench and all the dirt across into these shacks. I noticed a smell of burning plastic. I asked what it was, and they told me people would scavenge in the rubbish to find electrical cables, then burn off the plastic coating and sell the wire underneath for 30p a day.

They took me and Harry into this little tent where they were having a naming ceremony for a tiny baby. Considering where

she was living, she was actually dressed in some nice white clothes – they'd somehow got her some lovely things to wear. She was lying on a single mattress on the floor inside the tent and we went in to meet her dad. He shook our hands, then turned to Harry and said, 'Please, please take my baby away with you. She needs a better life. Please take her away from here.' I was just gutted. It was really hard. In fact it was the hardest thing I've ever had to listen to in my life. I just couldn't deal with it.

We also met a guy who'd been trained to be a cook with money raised by Comic Relief. He was only making outdoor street food, but he was cooking nonetheless and providing for the whole community – as well as earning a wage – as a result of the training. That's the only way things are gonna change there.

The whole Ghana trip was a reality check, big time. When you've seen stuff like that it's hard to feel sorry for yourself on a long bus journey away from your family on the way to another sold-out gig.

When I think of the scale of our second album tour it's hard to comprehend, even now. In the end we played in the region of 130 shows. That's ridiculous! I can't believe we genuinely did that many shows, and the fact we even had the opportunity is such a huge thing. Better still, the crowds were always amazing. There's a lot of homesickness and missing friends and family on the road, of course. We were still only young lads who'd recently moved away from home, and now suddenly we were off halfway round the world. So I'm not gonna lie. There have been times on tour when I've struggled

It's hard to believe that I was only 17 when one Direction started. that feels like a different lifetime to me now — so much has happened since this band began.

– you'd be a liar if you were to say it was always perfectly fine. Then one of the lads would say something, or do something stupid and make me laugh, and I'd be fine again. We were just getting used to life on the road, I guess. Later, in 2013, when I realised I couldn't go to my granddad's funeral because I'd got a gig in Australia, that hit home and really hurt.

I'm really aware that the success of One Direction has taken me away from home and my family prematurely. I was only 17 when this all started on *The X Factor*, after all. It has played with my mum's head a fair bit. It's hard for her and Dad to understand sometimes. There are so many things in my life that are perfectly normal to me, but they – understandably – aren't able to comprehend or grasp them. They do sometimes say, 'We don't know how you deal with some of the issues, Liam,' but you just learn, don't you? I've had to be so independent from a young age, and I haven't experienced that period of my life with my parents where they watched me grow up into a young man. I don't get to spend too much time at home – I do go back quite a lot but not as much as I'd like. It was quite a bit for them to take in. I actually think in a way it was much harder for them than it was for me, because I'm always around other people during the day. But for my parents, it must have been a very strange thing to suddenly not have me in the house.

However, being in One Direction has brought some massive benefits to my life. The biggest upsides for me are being able to give my family a good life and things they can enjoy doing, a nicer house and the fact that they don't really have to worry about when the next cheque is coming in. Mind you, my dad still works every single day! He goes months

without having a day off and is proud of that fact. He's a working-class man and loves going out to his job. Nothing will ever change for my parents in that sense, and if Dad stops work he'll be bored.

I can see bits and pieces of that work ethic in myself, which I've obviously picked up from my parents. If I hadn't made a go of my singing then I might well have followed Dad into an apprenticeship at his factory. Although I'm in this massive band, have a nice house and can in theory buy anything I want or go anywhere in the world, I like being at work 'cos it's something I enjoy doing. I also like the fact that we make a physical product – the fact that we record a song and it becomes part of an album. Maybe that's a working-class idea too. I enjoy putting my earphones on and listening to what we have all created.

Something else that being in One Direction has given me is lots of amazing new friendships. I've been lucky enough to meet some incredible people along the way. Sometimes I don't think I have that many friends – but you don't need that many, just a few special ones. You do get to meet some really interesting characters.

Getting back to the second album tour, it all started off with multiple gigs at the O2. I found that pretty bizarre, to be honest. I've been to watch a couple of shows there, such as JLS, and it was a gig that we'd always aimed to go and do. It's a beautiful place to play. Whenever I go there and I'm watching someone else's show it makes me really wanna play there again. When I was younger there was a chance to go on a school trip to the Millennium Dome, as it was called back in the day. I wanted to go but my sister fancied it as well, and we couldn't afford for both of us to go. I was just a dippy kid back then, and my parents thought Ruth would remember and appreciate the day more because she was older. So I never got to go. I was gutted. I remember when she came back she said, 'I've got you a present from London.' She'd bought me a Dome-shaped pencil sharpener. So I did chuckle a little to myself when we played there, as I got to the Millennium Dome in the end!

There's so much to take in every single day when you're in One Direction, which is absolutely amazing, and we feel very lucky. Occasionally, it has a personal impact that you don't expect. Sometimes when I'm on my own or hanging out I find myself unable to do normal things. I can't seem to switch off, and if I do have a day off I get bored and then a bit sad 'cos I feel like I'm not doing enough. *What more can I do today?* It kinda does mess you around. I just can't sit still for more than ten minutes. The only thing we've known for the last four years is get up and go, go, go! Add that to the way I was hyper when I was a kid and it makes me very restless.

Sometimes it stops me sleeping too. I might find out some band news during the day if we have a Number 1 or something else exciting, and I lie in bed thinking about it for hours. I often find myself looking out of windows or from balconies just having a good think. To be honest, I'm terrible for not going to sleep. I'm always just contemplating what I have to do next or what else I can do, and end up thinking about so many different things for hours, sometimes till it's almost morning. I simply don't sleep very much. How can I with a hundred million things going on in my head? Mind you, when I finally do drift off I can sleep for hours. It just takes me a while to clock off!

I've noticed being in the band seems to have affected me in other ways too. I am pretty confident mostly. However, I seem to have started to struggle with my confidence when it comes to some really mundane things, such as going shopping. I don't go shopping that often, to be fair, but when I do I sometimes get quite nervous about buying something or trying something on. Mostly I'm absolutely fine but other times I can feel a little self-conscious. Occasionally it's the same if I go into a bar – I find myself just standing there not shouting up. I just get nervous about standing out, I guess. I don't know why that is, as I can happily stand in front of 50,000 people with the other boys and chat away and then perform with them, but for some reason I occasionally find it quite nerve-wracking to do certain everyday things. That's crazy, isn't it?

You have to watch yourself around people too, because this job can make you very self-obsessed if you're not careful. Some stars have people looking after them all day, every day, and they're in interviews talking about themselves all the time. You can get into bad habits – for example, I had a phase of jumping in on conversations because I'd have some really exciting news about the band and I couldn't wait to tell people. I'd interrupt, I wouldn't take enough notice of what was going on in other people's lives and I was rubbish at listening. I'd jump in halfway through someone else's sentence and say, 'Hey, guess what ...?!' or whatever, interrupting them with some news about the band. You've gotta watch out for that. You need to keep that sense of perspective.

then
and
now

I'm still no good at chatting up girls, but then that's always been the case! I've always enjoyed having girlfriends and have been lucky enough to not be single for that long. When I was a kid I'd ask a lot of girls out at school. My mates used to pretend a girl liked me so that I'd ask her out and get turned down! Now when I'm out and I see a girl in a club I usually can't find the courage to go and talk to her ... I get nervous, really bad.

I also worry about whether I've spent too much money on something or not given enough to my family or whether I should or shouldn't buy a house. These are all very big decisions that sometimes feel like they're coming at me too fast, too young. Early on I used to look forward to having a big house, but I wanted to do the Uni/student stage of having a flat first. So I did that and got a lovely flat in London. Now I'm looking forward to picking a house that I might spend a lot of years in – but I'm only 21, so it's kinda weird to be making these decisions. I worry about making mistakes with things like this. It's nerve-wracking and a bit of a minefield sometimes. I always over-think absolutely every single detail. When I was at school I'd hear it at parents' evenings: 'He over-thinks,' rather than just keeping it simple. I'm still learning a lot about life and what I want from it. With all this worry I can be my own worst enemy.

Back at the O2 our friend Ben Winston, together with Morgan Spurlock, started filming us for what would become our first movie, *This Is Us*. I'm *so* glad we did that film. With One Direction it's easy to forget so much about what's happening to us. Sometimes loads happens in 24 hours, and it's hard to remember that individual day – never mind the day or week or month before. That's why I feel so lucky that we made the movie. It's an amazing document of our experiences.

Having the cameras on us for so long was difficult at times, especially if we wanted to chill out, but you have to kinda just roll with it. Besides, we all knew it was the biggest opportunity for One Direction, such an amazing thing for us to do. Even if someone came and made a movie just for us five for when we're older, that would be sick, but the fact that so many people wanted to see it and understand us a bit more was a privilege.

I actually haven't watched the full movie yet! There was so much going on, and then when we went to the cinema for the première they pulled us out halfway through to go and do promo. So I'm really looking forward to the day when I'm old and grey and I can sit down with my kids and a bag of popcorn and say, 'Come on, kids, this is what I was like when I was your age!'

I've been lucky enough to have met some pretty famous celebrities and that's a really fun part of my job. I don't like to chat to celebrities too much because at the end of the day I'm a fan myself. I do get nervous meeting these people, plus I'm anxious not to get too much in their face. Our job does create amazing opportunities to meet people, though – starting with Robbie Williams, way back obviously, then people like Michael Bublé (my first ever gig!), even the Queen! So it can all get a bit weird. You've gotta know when to keep it low-key, I think. When we met Will Smith I just said, 'Hello,

the guys doing some interviews

I'm a big fan.' I didn't wanna stand there and say, 'Ah, Will, matey, how's the wife and kids?!'

A few big names stand out, such as David Beckham. He was really cool. We were at some party and he was there too. I sat and had a chat with him, and he was sound. Next time I met Beckham I'd gone to watch a film called *Class of '92*, which Ben Winston, our producer, was involved with. I walked in and there he was on the other side of the room. Amazingly, he clocked me and ... you know when lads give each other the nod? Well, I gave him the nod, he gave me the nod back, then to my shock he came straight over and said, 'Hey, how are you doing, Liam?' and shook my hand! I was like, *This is mad! David Beckham just gave me the nod from the other side of the room. That's sick!* I tell all my mates this story.

Another favourite celeb of mine is Pharrell Williams. What a nice guy! I got the opportunity to write with him one time when we were in the US and I was like, *I'm 100% going! I'm not missing this!* I went to the studio and I was sitting there in a chair, waiting. I was so nervous. It was the first session I'd ever done by myself and it was with one of the biggest music producers in the world. He's still drilling out tunes, getting more massive every year. Every time I see him now he'll come up to me and give me a hug and ask me how's it going, and he wants us to go back in the studio. That's a real buzz.

I'm also a huge fan of Michael McIntyre. He's just hilarious. I used to do a mean impression of him! We did the Pride of Britain Awards one time and he was there, and as soon as we walked in he started cracking jokes, 100 miles an hour. He was so funny. We got talking, I said, 'I'm a huge fan,' and we swapped numbers. He said, 'I want you to come to a show and I'm going to take the mickey out of you all night if you do!' When he texts me he calls me 'One of the Directions'. He cracks me up all the time. I always think, This is weird! I used to sit and watch his DVDs at home and now he's texting me . . . I haven't got the courage to go to a show yet, though!

Someone put it to me that other people might see me in the same way – as a celebrity – but that's not what we're about at all. We're well known for being in One Direction, I understand that, but most of the time I don't realise the extent of our profile, to be fair. We do a lot of meet-and-greets with fans – you see the look on some people's faces who can't really say anything, and they're breathing fast and they're all nervous. But I can't really associate that with me. Even though I know it's because they're meeting us, somehow it doesn't stack up.

I forget sometimes that my face is well known. I stay in my house a lot now because sometimes the reaction in public can be a bit intense. Me and my mate Paddy tried to go to Westfield shopping centre the other day, and I forgot that the schools were off for the holidays. We lasted about 20 minutes, then had to leave. Of course, I don't see myself as a celebrity . . . but I can see people staring, and I can sense them looking at me, gearing themselves up to come over and ask me a question or for a photo.

Part of this inability to see ourselves as well known or famous is because I still think we're normal lads in our early twenties, having a laugh. To be honest, the stuff we get up to is just the sort of stuff any bunch of 20-something lads would do if they got the chance. If you said to any 20-year-old lad, 'You can have full-size football goals wherever you go, ride quad bikes, go-karts, you can mess about, you can run away from people who are telling you to do more work,' he'd obviously say 'Yes!' Yes!' Who wouldn't do all this if they were lucky enough to be in that position? I'm just here to have a laugh.

The first single from our third album was 'Best Song Ever', which was a great tune and a fun video to make. During that period, though, easily the most daunting thing we had to do for promo was 1D Day. We had to broadcast online for about seven hours, and as none of us had ever presented a TV show before we didn't really know what to do! I'd been given all these sheets of script and directions, but to be honest I hadn't done enough revision so the management were a bit worried! I was like, 'I haven't really got a clue what I'm doing here, lads!' However, we made a go of it, and as I always say, 'When have we ever let you down?' We always get through these things somehow! Mind you, it was quite nerve-wracking because we were well aware of how many people were watching on the other side of the camera. Once we got into it we were fine, though, and even during my breaks I was just stuck to the telly watching it myself! That was a lot of fun. A good day, and we'll have to do it again and make it even better!

By the time we came to release our third album we'd become quite heavily involved in the songwriting itself. That was a big step up, all a part of us becoming more creative. When *Midnight Memories* went straight in at Number 1 in so many countries it was another big moment for us lads. We take nothing for granted, and because that album was very personal to us, seeing it do so well was a real vindication of our creative input.

In the future I'd absolutely love to be a songwriter. That way I can stay in the industry and still challenge myself to write great songs, have hits and be around a job that I've loved. I don't ever want to let this sort of thing go. There are so many stories of boy bands that have come and gone. A while ago there was a guy who came round to do Niall's roof and he used to be in a very successful boy band. I'm not going to say who it was, but I was just thinking, *He had success. He did really well. How did he go from there to fixing roofs?*

I'm worried about the idea of failing outside of this band. Songwriting really appeals to me because it's something I absolutely love, something that's a challenge and something that's very creative. There would be less attention on my life too, of course, but mainly I'd just love to wake up every day and write songs. I've been lucky enough that my dream comes true every day, so in the future I need to make sure I enjoy the benefits of that and also keep challenging myself. So, yes, I do worry about what might happen after this band, but perhaps that's only natural.

Some people in this band are super, *super* driven. Some people have said I'm very driven, but I see it more as I just like to make the most of my time and I like to do stuff. I don't know if I'd put myself in the 'super-driven' bracket, 'cos I do consider myself to be a bit lazy with certain things. Some-times I need to sort my priorities out a bit. That's why I get a

Backstage
ping-pong
#kansas city

liam

Liam

HONESTLY?
THE WHOLE
EXPERIENCE
HAS BEEN
MY FAVOURITE
MOMENT

bit worried if I get to the end of a day and don't feel like I've worked hard enough. It was always the same with my course work when I was a kid. I actually think our work ethic from school has carried on into being in this band. When I went to college to study music technology I worked really hard and got distinctions in everything, except one subject. But I always felt like I could do more – and I still get that feeling every day. Maybe with One Direction that's because I know we're in a very fortunate position and I never want to take anything for granted.

I wouldn't be able to say why I deserve to be in this position. I'm sure there are many people out there more talented than me, but for some reason I've kinda ended up here. You just have to make the most of it all, and that's why we're trying to make the band better the whole time. We owe it to ourselves – and to all our fans – to do that.

Life in One Direction just seems to get more and morecrazy. After we had a three-month break at the start of 2014 we came back at the Brit Awards and it was just completely crazy again. Instantly. Like we'd never been away. The momentum just seems to constantly ramp up and up. So many amazing times. People often ask me what is my favourite moment from being in One Direction.

Honestly? The whole experience has been my favourite moment.

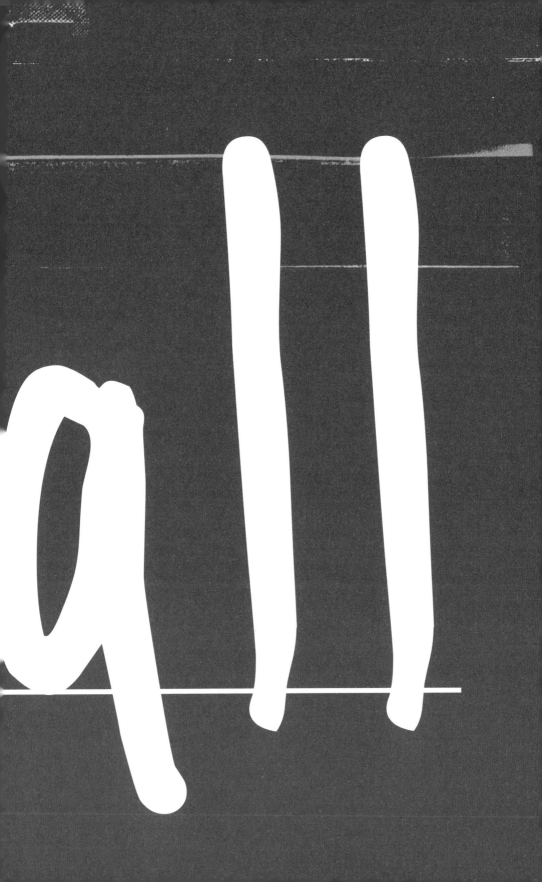

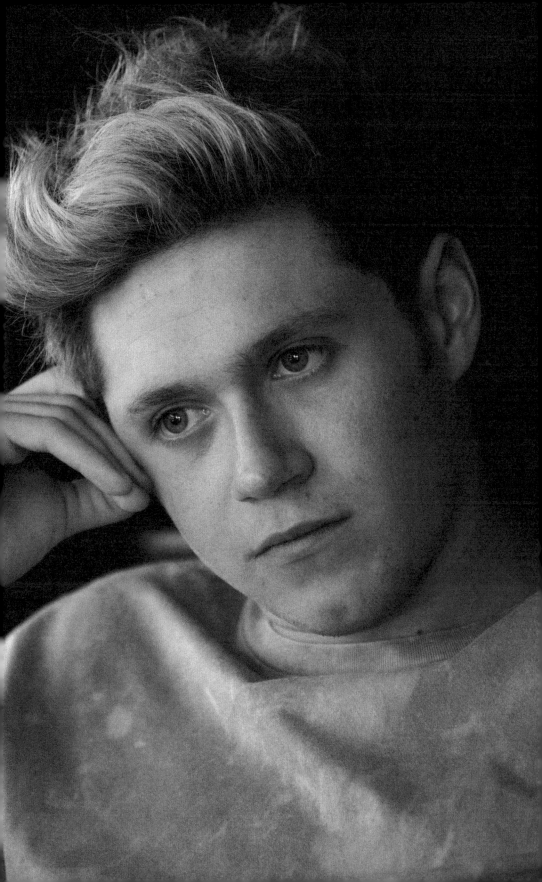

Sometimes I wonder how my childhood has prepared me for the madness that's One Direction. On the one hand, there's no preparing for this, certainly not on the scale the band has grown to. But I can see how certain things in my early years have helped. For starters, I was very independent from a young age. My parents separated when I was five, so I know how some kids find it hard if their parents aren't together. Obviously, it was upsetting from that point of view, but at the same time I felt like I had the best of both worlds, living between two houses. I've no complaints. I had a childhood that everyone else who lived near me wanted to have. I went to a good primary school, a good secondary school and had a laugh with the lads. It was grand, and I was a very happy kid. Yes, I messed about at school quite a bit, but I was just having the best time.

My mum lived out in the country, so I eventually decided to make my way back into town to live with Dad 'cos I had friends there. He used to work nights, so I ended up doing a lot of stuff for myself. My dad looked after me, obviously, but I also enjoyed doing my own washing and getting myself ready for school. People used to say to me, 'You're old before your years.' That sense of independence was really useful later on when One Direction started and suddenly in my mid-teens I was thrown into this mad world of living away from home.

From a really early age my dad would always take me to football matches in England. I think I was only four when I went to my first game. So I got used to travelling – which is helpful in this job! Really early on Saturday mornings he'd be like, 'Wake up, Niall. We've got to be on the boat from Dublin

Teeth all over the place in my last official primary-school photo.

at five this morning!' So I'd stumble out of bed and we'd somehow make the ferry to Holyhead, then jump on the train to Llandudno, across to Crewe, and catch the train from Crewe to Derby. I loved that journey and going to watch football with my dad. Looking back, I do think all that travelling at such a young age has helped me cope with the massive amount of flying and driving we do in the band.

Of course, the most obvious aspect of my childhood that has influenced my role in the band is my lifelong love of music. Funnily enough, there isn't really much musical history in my family – my parents didn't perform or have amateur singing careers, but they were really big music fans. I vividly remember two pivotal gigs that hugely influenced me – both by The Eagles. I went to see them twice before I was even ten. That was a pretty big deal for me, and I said, 'Dad, that was just the best night ever. I want to be able to sing like that!' The first concert I ever went to was McFly, then my second was The Eagles. Two totally different ends of the spectrum.

After that I was hooked, and I just wanted to get up on stage. Whether it was the choir or local productions like *Oliver!*, talent shows or busking – anything to do with performing – I just wanted to get up there and perform, even though I was crapping myself with nerves. I had a phase of wanting to do sound engineering too, front of house at venues. I went to so many gigs 'cos my dad's such a big music fan. I was always fascinated by how the sound was mixed, even though I didn't have a clue how they actually did it. I saw music as a way to broaden my horizons too – it seemed like it was offering up a chance to travel and see the world. So I guess you could look back on all of these parts of my childhood and say they either influenced my decisions to want to get into a band later in life or helped me once I joined One Direction.

My childhood was actually cut short by *The X Factor* because after One Direction took off I didn't even get the chance to finish my exams. I once said that for the first audition, 'I packed up everything in my life in a bag.' That's completely true. But what I didn't realise at the time when I was stuffing clothes into my little suitcase was that, pretty much, I was leaving home for good. After One Direction got put together, I was just shuttling between Ireland and England for the rest of the show. Then it was Judges' Houses and on to the live finals, after which I went home one more time, re-packed the suitcase . . . and I haven't lived in Ireland since. It was a case of grabbing some clothes, slinging my guitar over my shoulder and off I went.

I think one year I was home for 26 days in total – not all at the same time! Let's be clear, though. I'm not complaining. I never really get homesick – I don't know what it is. I miss my family and friends really badly sometimes, but luckily I've got my cousin here in London and I always have people around me, especially 'cos all of us in the band live near each other. So I can always have a bit of a laugh. If I'm feeling down I can pretty quickly find someone to have a chat with and a bit of banter. I tend to go around annoying people, just chatting away. Plus the best way to ease any homesickness is just to think of One Direction – I'm mad into this band.

Moving to a big city wasn't such a shock for me. My mum obviously asked me if I felt all right about the move and I was

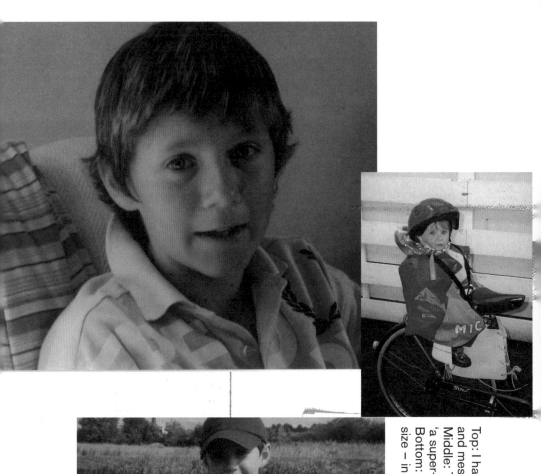

Top: I have extremely fond memories of my childhood – playing and messing about with my mates. It was pretty idyllic.

Middle: This wasn't exactly what I had in mind when I asked for 'a super-fast road bike'.

Bottom: By the time I got home, this fish had grown to twice the size – in my mind, at least.

Top: With my brother Greg and Mum, Maura.

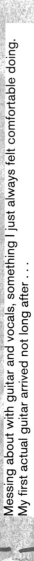

Messing about with guitar and vocals, something I just always felt comfortable doing.
My first actual guitar arrived not long after . . . .

like, 'Yeah, I'll be grand. I can't wait!' Even though I was coming from a town where everyone knows each other, hands down starting from scratch in London wasn't a problem. I'd been there quite a few times to watch football with Dad and I was ready for the challenge. I was so excited too. How could I not be?

While I settled into London easily enough, the minute I moved over it was 'Lights, camera, action!' every Saturday on the biggest show in the country. That took some getting used to! Nothing can prepare you for *The X Factor*. You're straight in there, cameras in your face pretty much 24/7. BANG! From the minute you wake up to the minute you go to sleep, there are studios, rehearsals, interviews, rushing around all over the place during the week, then Saturday's show . . . BOOM! By Sunday you're wrecked, and then it just starts all over again. What a buzz, though!

I remember very clearly the first day after *The X Factor* finished. Along with Matt Cardle and Rebecca Ferguson, we were the last people in a ten-bedroom house – this mad, messy, huge house. None of us boys in the band had packed but we had to be out of the house by 11am. Then we got a rap on the door. It was our new tour manager, Paul, this big Irish fella who comes walking into the room and goes, 'Right, lads. I'm Paul. You've got half an hour to get packed!'

We went to the K West Hotel in Shepherd's Bush and had some lunch. We were all really excited but at the same time we were like, 'What's gonna happen next? Where are we going today? What are we going to do?' How could we tell? We didn't even have a record deal, although it had kinda been suggested to us that we might be offered one.

Then we found out that Zayn's granddad had died. Talk about contrast. What a shame for Zayn. So we all jumped into a car and drove up to Bradford to go to his granddad's funeral. Zayn was brilliant. Once he'd looked after his family situation he just snapped back into being with the band. I don't know how he did it. Then we came back down to London and went into the Sony offices a couple of days later. We walked in, and they sat us down in this boardroom and said they wanted to sign us. I was just sitting there thinking, *This is sick!*

It was really noticeable how all of us got on so quickly. We always had a good laugh, and the relationship between the five lads in the band just kinda happened. We spent every single day with each other and never really fell out. Sure, there were a couple of niggles here and there – but that's bound to happen. Our first PA tour of small clubs was a crucial part of us starting to become a unit, driving up and down the country in a small tour bus, performing all these club gigs, a couple of bar mitzvahs, all that. It was mainly great reactions, but we played a dodgy club in Leeds one night and they started throwing things and eventually booed us off stage!

Luckily, that was the exception and it all took off from there. The first six months of One Direction was just nuts. As soon as we got to venues, TV studios or radio stations, people would say, 'There's loads of girls by the gate, a few hundred maybe.' So we'd go out, chat with them and try to meet as many as possible. In a pretty short space of time, though, the numbers grew and grew, and people started saying, 'There's a few thousand . . .'

I was a keen sportsman as a kid – golf, football and Gaelic football – fortunately at this point I didn't have a crocked knee!

0-2276-503

When we were on *The X Factor* we all thought it was hard work – and it was, to be fair. But as soon as we left the show and got out there on our own, the work-rate just went mad, totally crazy. We were being shepherded around all over the place and everyone wanted a bit of us. I don't mind admitting that a part of me was thinking, *Right, you have got six months to do as much as you can. Chances are it's all gonna be over after that.* I think that was probably a realistic way to be, and it certainly meant I never slacked off or took my opportunity for granted. Obviously we've managed to last a little longer than six months and we've had a good bit of success, but back then we didn't know if each gig might be our last. We just thought we had nothing to lose because no one knew what to expect from us. At that stage we were like, 'Let's have a bit of a laugh, let's make this as good as we can!' Looking back, those were the days! Great craic, like!

My excitement ramped up when we flew to LA and then Sweden for the début album recording sessions. That was amazing. I'd been to New York and Boston before, but Zayn had only ever been on a plane once, for Judges' Houses, and we'd told him all sorts, like, 'The plane is gonna loop the loop and do all these mad stunts, Zayn!' He was freaking out, it was hilarious! When we arrived at LAX airport we were shocked to see a few fans, but we kinda dismissed it. We were like, 'Nah, that can't be ...' We were all buzzing, enjoying the weather, going in and out the studios, the most relaxed it's ever been. In LA they didn't start till 4pm so we sat outside by the pool for hours. It was great.

I was so naïve to the whole studio world. We'd been in a studio very briefly for *The X Factor* winner's single session

#tbt
recording through the dark in
toronto, i think.

but that was so short. Now we were in LA for our own album sessions it was literally like, 'So, lads, what are these headphones for?' The studio mixing desk just looked like a table of gibberish to me. We were all so in awe of the producers too, they seemed to know so much and have written so many hit songs. The fact that you don't know the producers either is a bit weird, and singing in front of them felt a little bit like auditioning for *The X Factor* again. I was crapping myself and was saying to the lads, 'I hope they think what I'm doing is OK. These guys have recorded pretty much everyone who's anyone!' I wouldn't say I was the best singer in the world back then! In retrospect it was pretty straightforward actually – we were told, 'Go in and sing this line, then come out until later when you will sing this next line . . .'

We didn't have a clue, to be fair, and I'm kinda happy that we were directed back then because otherwise we wouldn't have had 'What Makes You Beautiful' and the great album that we did. We had good people around us who'd been in the industry for years and knew exactly what they were doing. We were still kids, plus we were super busy promoting and doing PAs and gigs, so we wouldn't have had the time to write songs even if we'd had the opportunity. That first album was so crucial as well, so it would've been too risky to let us loose with loads of writing. Everyone was waiting to see what we were gonna do now that we were off the show, what kind of music we were gonna make and how we'd sound.

Our horizons were soon to broaden too, as we had other overseas studios booked for our first recording sessions. The very early sessions in Sweden were really cool. On the first day in the studio we went for lunch and on our way back

there were these two Swedish girls standing by the studio entrance. We actually just walked straight past them because we didn't realise they were there to see us. They shouted out to us, 'Do you mind if we get your autographs and a few photos, please?' We were obviously like, 'Of course, no bother!' but at the same time we were like, 'Where have you guys come from?' and we found out they'd taken a long train journey through most of Sweden to get there. We were just gobsmacked. That was our first taste of fans outside the UK.

On our first day recording in Sweden there were literally just those two fans outside, but as each day went by there were more and more girls waiting to meet us, and by the end of that week the entire road outside the studio was closed off because there were hundreds of fans everywhere. It was mayhem.

Then the chaos and crazy interest in the band started to spread all over Europe. The record label would sort out days for fans to get wristbands and come in, and we'd sing a few songs and maybe do a signing. It was always mental. We'd never seen anything like it in our lives.

As you know, our first single didn't come out till the September after *The X Factor*. In the nine months before that we basically slogged it out in the back of a Mercedes van, in and out of hotels, the *X Factor* tour, time in studios, radio stations, video shoots and doing photo shoots. We brought out a book, did a load of signings, and we must have done every teen magazine in the world. When it was apparent that we were becoming big in Europe – our fans are amazing! – we had to start doing European promo too. The band's horizon seemed to be getting bigger and bigger every day.

Santiago!

Sitting here looking back, it's actually hard to think of everything that went on. It's so difficult to remember, it was all such a blur.

I know our début single might seem like an age ago, but I do remember at the time that people were impressed. There was a feeling that it was a really good-quality pop song and that we'd made a great start. Obviously the Number 1 spot was a crazy start to our career, but to be honest we were working so hard we only briefly celebrated it, quick pat on the back like, and then BANG!, on to the next thing. It was relentless. I was so excited every day, and those were amazing times. I turned 18 in that September, and around that period we played a gig to a really bad audience, a supermarket buying team who were totally disinterested. What a way to reach that milestone!

After the début single came out the band just went through the roof. Whatever our definition of crazy had been before was now completely rewritten – it moved on to a whole other level. We never really got time to wipe our arse after that.

I've tried to analyse *why* One Direction went so completely mental. I like to think that if it was just about the music, and if no other factors were involved, we'd still be a popular band with a great fanbase, because in my opinion we've made some great songs. But I'm also realistic and I know it's not just about the music – there's marketing, social media, record-label schedules – so many things you can't possibly be aware of before you first get involved in a band.

There's no doubt that our fans had a huge part to play in our early success. Specifically, our presence on social media was key. The fans took to that so well and it just created

this colossal word of mouth about One Direction that was like a wildfire spreading around the globe. I think they knew then – and still do now – that our own accounts are genuine. They know that what we are saying is our own thoughts, our own words. No managers text me to say, 'You need to tweet something today, Niall ...' I just do it all of my own accord. I think that created a real intimacy with the fans from day one that they appreciated and enjoyed, so once they got involved too the effect was just unbelievable. I think it's hard to put your finger on the exact reasons for those early months when the band blew up, but whatever they were, something crazy was happening with One Direction. It wasn't so much like being inside a bubble as being blown off the floor by a whirlwind.

Our first album, *Up All Night,* was a good pop record, in my opinion. OK, I might not play it much these days but then I think a lot of artists would probably say that about their earliest work, if they were being totally honest. As I've said, we didn't get overly involved in the writing but we still felt a personal connection with the record, and going out there to perform it was such a buzz. When it went into the UK charts at Number 2 and even to Number 1 in 17 countries, I just couldn't believe what was happening. I knew we were working hard, I knew there was a buzz around the band that was perhaps quite infectious, I knew the fans were just out of this world helping us, but it was still a big shock to me. I thought, *Maybe this is going to last more than six months after all.*

I think that it was the early PAs and then the headline tour for the first album that really cemented One Direction

together as five mates on this mad quest around the world. That's when the chemistry really started. We'd had that week at Harry's step-dad's bungalow, which had helped a lot, but the first PA tour really fuelled that relationship between us all too. We've had the same bus driver for all these years, a Scouse fella called Don, and he was there on that first tour. In fact we've kept quite a few of the same crew all the way along this crazy journey.

The first gig ever on our own was in Watford Coliseum, which is like the size of a small bedroom – it's a modest town hall, basically. The crowd reaction was just ridiculous, all a bit mad. I remember that show really clearly, as well as saying to the lads during the gig, 'This place is mad! The fans are going nuts!' We were going round doing these gigs, sleeping on the same tour bus and being together every day of the week. We were lads in our late teens and I was like, 'Lads, this is the best time of our lives!' How could it not be?

One Direction just seemed to scale up so quickly. We'd been shocked when we found out we were popular round those PA club nights in the UK, then we'd been even more amazed that we already had a following in Europe. Then, weirdest of all, we went to the States – pretty much as five lads just having a laugh and seeing where it took us – and the whole thing just completely blew up.

To be fair, we didn't actually have many expectations when we flew out for the first US promo trip. Yes, we knew it was a big deal to go over there, but you just don't expect success. Why would you? You hear of so many bands going out there and trying so hard but ultimately failing. The way we looked at it was, 'Let's just go out there, have a bit of fun, be ourselves,

work hard, do every promo we can do, see what happens ...'
Back then we only had one security guy – Paul again! – who
used to come everywhere with us. We started off not expecting anything, just us five and Paul in a small van, everywhere
we went.

It's hard to pinpoint any single moment during the first US
promo trip when I realised something ridiculous was going
on. The *Big Time Rush* tour was a crazy time when we just
couldn't comprehend how all these American fans were singing every word of every song back at us. We'd often be
sitting in the back of the bus after a show and everyone would
be just looking a bit dazed, and then one of the lads would
say, 'What the hell is going on here?' I kept thinking to myself,
*I could be back at school now and yet here I am on tour in
the States.*

'What Makes You Beautiful' getting into the Top 30 in the
States was also amazing. Hearing that our début album had
been brought forward a week because of the intense interest
in us was pretty cool too. But having thousands of fans turn
up to cheer us on in the street before we went on the *Today*
show was just on another level. That programme had been
built up to be the biggest thing, but to be perfectly honest
we didn't really know much about it 'cos we're not American.
We later found out some of the fans had been queueing overnight in the freezing-cold New York streets. How can you ever
thank people for that?

Seeing so many people in the streets of New York was
just the most surreal experience – it's hard to describe. One
of my earliest memories as a kid is going there on holiday to
see my aunt, so New York has a special place in my life. Then

hearing about the sheer numbers at the *Today* show, 10,000 fans, all those people who went to so much trouble to come and see us, we were so pleased. After that, any thoughts of the band struggling to get a profile in the States went out of the window. The rest of the year was nuts: the tour over there, more TV, radio, promo – everywhere we went the fans just went crazy.

Oddly enough, if I'm being totally honest with you, going to perform on a TV show is when I get the most nervous. In fact, I get so tense I'm often close to puking. I'm not lying – I can get physically sick. Even now, after all the experience I've had with TV, it just kills me. We started off on a TV show so I should be most at home there, but every time we do telly it riddles me with nerves. With TV, I'm petrified from the minute I get ready in the dressing room to the second we walk out onto the set. I don't know why that is and, to be honest with you, it's getting worse, not better. I think I get in such a nervous state that it just spirals into this one massive bag of nerves. Then when the next TV show is coming along, the apprehension hits immediately and it all starts again, only even worse. Maybe it's because it feels quite intimate? I don't like singing in front of small crowds. If you ask me to sing at a party in front of friends – not a chance! – but put me on a stage in front of 50,000 people and I'll sing my heart out, relaxed as you like. I understand this doesn't really make sense, but I'm just telling it as it is.

Even in 2013, when we were invited to perform at the American Music Awards, I was in such a state about singing a song I was usually totally comfortable with. To be fair, it was made worse by the nature of the artists on the show. Just

Niall

WE LATER FOUND OUT SOME OF THE FANS HAD BEEN QUEUEING OVERNIGHT IN THE FREEZING-COLD NEW YORK STREETS.

HOW CAN YOU EVER THANK PEOPLE FOR THAT?

before we went out to perform, Justin Timberlake was coming off after collecting an award and I remember looking at him and saying to the lads, 'Is that the calibre of people that are here tonight?' I scanned the crowd from the side of stage and I could see Lady Gaga sitting in the front row, Justin was over there and Katy Perry was a few rows away from him. It was ridiculous! That was just in the theatre, never mind the tens of millions of people watching at home! I was like, 'Crap!'

To make matters worse, as he walked off Justin Timberlake came over to say hello and I was absolutely bricking it by then, nearly swallowing my own puke. I just said, 'I think I'm gonna puke, lads.' I was fine in the end, I did the song OK, but it's pretty draining being that nervous.

I'll never forget the moment when I found out *Up All Night* had hit Number 1 in the States. We were in New York doing some promo and had hammered every radio station, every TV show, every meet-and-greet, everything we could possibly throw ourselves at. I was actually in the back of a taxi with my friend going to the Sony offices to collect basketball tickets for a Knicks game when I got a phonecall off Will, our manager. He said, 'I've got some news for you, Niall,' in this really droll tone. Then he said, 'Well, it could've been better . . .' and I was like, 'Ah, crap!' but then he said, 'You're Number 1!' Me and my friend were absolutely boxing the face off each other in the back of this taxi, so much so that the driver kicked us out because he didn't know what the hell was going on.

Once we were at Number 1 in the States we soon realised what we thought was mental was just small on the future scale of all things One Direction. The more busy we are the

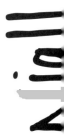

We've even got our own interview room!

better it suits me, honest to God. I've the attention span of a goldfish, honestly, and I'm the most fidgety person in the world. I've probably played with my phone about ten times in the last ten seconds writing this, without me even knowing. So I enjoy my life being manic, and rushing about all over the place.

The big tour to promote that first album was something else. Some of the venues in the States were modest theatres but one night we turned up and it was a shed with seats for 8,000 and a big lawn area at the back. We asked, 'What's that lawn area for?' and they said, 'We always sell tickets for that area on the day ... so you can expect another 25,000 people to turn up for the show.'

Around that time we also met Michelle Obama, and I have to say she was unbelievable. Her daughters were lovely too, chatting away and occasionally saying, 'My dad said this ...' or 'My dad did that ...' like any kids would, but because they're such normal kids you almost have to remind yourself that they're talking about the President. They're the most humble people ever and were made to be the President's daughters. They can chat with anyone and have obviously been brought up really well. You only have to meet their mum to see that – Michelle is amazing, a lovely woman. We've never met the President but he's been in contact saying thank you for sorting his girls out with tickets and all that. I'm a huge Obama fan – I even have a statue of him in my back garden!

That début album tour went on for ages 'cos we just kept getting dates added and added. Yes, it was tiring and at one point or another all of us were exhausted. We eventually did over 60 dates, so that was inevitable. But what a buzz! Crazy.

On tour you just have to remind yourself that you're all in the same boat. We would say to ourselves, 'I can't go home but neither can that sound engineer over there; our tour manager can't get home either, all our security, management, crew ...' That's just the way we always looked at it – we're all in it together. We were so privileged to have the chance to get out there and show that our record sales were not just hype, that we had a live show to back the album up. We've always wanted to work as hard as we can at justifying the press and public interest in One Direction.

While this was all kicking off, we were also writing for our second album. I personally felt the pressure on that record was huge. Before we did the first album there was no pressure really ... well, there was a bit but not as much, because people didn't know us. I honestly felt like we'd nothing to lose. But with the début album hitting Number 1 all over the place, now we had to better ourselves. There was a change in the atmosphere now that there were some pretty serious expectations. And because we were so busy we had to find time somewhere to record and write – but we were also on the road, so working that much meant it wasn't always easy to find it. We used to talk about it together, trying to figure out a way to get the album done: 'How are we gonna find a place to get this new song recorded? Maybe start in that hotel tomorrow? If not, then we aren't gonna be free for days ...' That was how it developed.

There were so many mad events in 2012 I'm not sure which ones to look back on. Obviously the Olympics closing ceremony was a big moment for all of us. That was all a bit crazy, thinking – or trying not to think! – of billions of people watching around the world! The whole experience happened that quick, honestly. I remember walking into the backstage area and saying to the rest of the band, 'Lads! Madness are in the dressing room next to us!' They were brilliant. They're just lads from north London having a right laugh and were great. Ed Sheeran was there and Liam Gallagher was too, having a bit of a laugh with us.

'What Makes You Beautiful' was edited shorter to fit into one lap of the track so it was over super-fast. All I could see when we were singing was thousands of camera flashes, then before we knew it we were finished and backstage again, looking at each other. I said, 'Lads, did that just happen?' It's only when you watch shows like that back that you realise the scale of what you've just done.

When an album you've made goes to the Number 1 spot in 31 countries, to be honest it's just completely baffling. It was mad enough when *Up All Night* did so well internationally, but when the second album, *Take Me Home,* just blew up all over the world it was quite hard to take in. How can you not get a massive buzz off that? You will never get used to that feeling. I was obviously delighted and I was also pleased 'cos we'd worked so hard and it seemed to be paying off.

I've spoken about our gig at Madison Square Garden before but it's a really important landmark in the One Direction story. We had a new stage made for that show, we rehearsed hard in England then we went over to the States and did some small arena rehearsal shows before rocking up to MSG on the day. We were still so young and naïve, and in a way – and because we're not American – it was impossible

for us to fully comprehend the significance of that iconic US gig. I freely admit I didn't take it all in beforehand, but I tell you what, the moment I walked inside the actual venue it hit me like a truck. You just feel it. You get an instant vibe when you walk around that place and can sense the history. The nerves started kicking in then, and I don't mind admitting that we were bricking it. You see all these photos of Muhammad Ali fights, Sinatra and Elvis concerts, and if you watch our movie you can see us biting our nails – that stomach-churning feeling. We had to make that gig as good as possible. We owed that to ourselves, and to our fans, and also out of respect to the venue and its amazing history. What a night!

Playing Madison Square Garden was without a doubt one of the best experiences of my life. Going to Ghana with Comic Relief in February 2013 is also right up there. If you can still lose the plot and become a celebrity diva after going out to a place like that then you really are letting yourself down. It was a pretty extreme contrast – playing MSG, where we had thousands of people screaming at us, to flying into Ghana where absolutely no one had a clue who we were.

As soon as we arrived at the slum we were visiting there was this overpowering stench of poverty – just filth everywhere. It was, in a way, the most disgusting place on Earth, certainly in terms of what I'd ever seen. Yet it was also a really happy place. It was all such a culture shock, both ways really. We felt really bad even going back to the hotel for a shower. The people living there are just incredible and their spirit is mind-boggling. You can only try your best for them when you admire them so much. Our Comic Relief single, 'One Way Or Another', hit Number 1 in quite a few countries and raised

AMERICAN MUSIC AWARDS

2013

NOVEMBER 24, 2013
NOKIA THEATRE LA LIVE

O H S B
G M ● P
A T D R

ONE DIRECTION

Niall

over £1 million for the charity, so hopefully that money has helped improve their situation.

By mad contrast, that same month we started a major world tour, this time to promote the second album, *Take Me Home*, which would eventually stretch to around 130 gigs. I know this might sound a bit odd, but that tour was actually quite relaxed! We were doing arenas by now so quite often we didn't need to get to the venue till late in the afternoon, which meant we had a chance to chill out, catch up on sleep, relax a little – it was great! For a man who loves his sleep, that can only be good news – I do waste a lot of my life sleeping. 'Niall, wake up!' is a phrase I hear a lot on tour.

That felt like a proper tour to me. We had a little less promo and more time to try to record on the road. So we'd be sticking mattresses against hotel room walls, stuffing pillows everywhere to soundproof a room, just working off a laptop with a couple of speakers, a microphone – real basic stuff, but done properly it can really work. There's also a vibe on tour that you can sometimes capture in a song – you're all in this experience on the road together, which can come across in songs that you write and record while you're travelling.

Any spare second we had we'd write and write. Since we were on the road so much, I think maybe only one song on our third album was done entirely in the studio. We didn't record every day on tour, maybe once or twice a week. I would've liked to have played more guitar on the record too, but it just wasn't always possible. Sometimes recording so much on the road can be a killer on your voice, 'cos you'd get up in the morning after the gig the night before, head down to a local studio or more often than not use a makeshift recording set-up back at the hotel, record for maybe four or five hours, then off to the venue for a soundcheck, do the actual show, then back to bed and so on. You also really have to watch your drinking and eating, not going mad eating rubbish or boozing. It was quite a challenge, but we all just wanted to contribute to that album so much.

One of the maddest gigs for me was when we played an arena one night, and then the next evening my favourite band ever, The Eagles, played there and I got to meet them! I'm a huge fan. As far as melodies go it doesn't get better than them boys, so I listen to a lot of their stuff. That band gives you so many ideas as to the composition of a song and how it should go. As I said earlier, my dad was a huge fan of The Eagles and I'd seen them twice before I was even ten. When I went to see them in the US that night I was chatting away backstage to them, but I was really star-struck. How could I not be? It was The Eagles, for God's sake!

The whole notion of celebrity is a really weird concept to me. I get star-struck by certain people I meet through my job, so on the one hand I have to acknowledge that I admire some stars in that way, but when people tell me that they, or someone they know, are star-struck by me, I frankly find it completely absurd.

I remember when I first heard The Script. I loved their single 'The Man Who Can't Be Moved' and I used to sing it at various talent shows in Ireland. I assumed they were American, but then I found out they were Irish and it was all over! So fast-forward to 2014 and I'm sitting in a studio with The Script writing songs. It just baffles me. Same with Pearl Jam – I'm a massive fan of that band. We were in Seattle

119

in 2013 and the band's singer Eddie Vedder brought his kids to the show. His guitarist Mike McCready came up to me and said, 'Niall, do you mind if I get a picture please?' It was just so surreal. This was Pearl Jam! Then I walked out on stage and Eddie Vedder was standing right at the front of the arena, watching. I had to play guitar in front of the fella, and I don't think I've ever played better than that night – talk about pressure!

I obviously really enjoy these perks of my job but as I said, I can't see how people might feel the same way about me. It just doesn't add up. When I was recuperating from my knee injury – more of that in a minute! – I was invited to work with the physio team at Chelsea FC and I got along with the players really well – they were all sound, great craic. But a few of them were a little quiet around me and didn't seem to want to chat much. I was worried I'd maybe said something wrong and I was like, 'What's wrong with him? Is everything all right?' Eventually one of the coaches said, 'He's got two kids who are mad One Direction fans and he's a bit star-struck, Niall.' I think I swore when I heard that! Come on, really? Honestly, that's just crazy to think like that.

When we played Washington, DC, one of the biggest stars that's ever walked the Earth, Ronnie Wood came into our dressing room, then he came to our movie première. 'All right, lads, how's it going? I'm looking forward to seeing this film you've made.' Different league, like. It's always the most famous ones who seem the nicest, like Jay-Z, and Will Smith's unbelievable – he remembers everyone and there's no arrogance about him at all. Johnny Depp invited us round his house for a BBQ. *That* is someone proper famous.

I'll never see myself as a celebrity. That's someone who wants to be a celebrity, who's seen everywhere and gets papped every day of the week. You can stay away from paparazzi – I've done it for the last four years. You either want to be papped or you don't. I go and do my job, go home, then mostly sit in my house. I don't go on many holidays; I prefer to sit in my house, mostly. I might go to the pub, have a few pints and watch the football whenever I can – pretty much do the same thing I'd have done if I was at college back at home. Obviously we've earned a great living from the band, so I know I'm very lucky in that sense, but there's absolutely no reason why it should change who you are. I wouldn't say I was the flashest person in the world. I've a car and a nice house, but I'd say I've fairly simple tastes after that. Easy to look after. I'm not about to splash the cash and make a fool of myself. Besides, I'd do this job for a tenner, so I would.

Even if someone was to say I was a celebrity, I'd reply by saying I'm the worst celebrity in the world. A crap celebrity. I don't have any celebrity friends and I don't go out partying all the time. My day out is going to Tesco. I could go out every night if I wanted, and because of the perks of this job I could get into nightclubs and have a load of free drinks, but I'd rather pay four quid for a quiet pint up the road watching Sky Sports. People who want to do that whole party/celebrity life, let them do it. Each to their own, but that's not for me.

I'll tell you a story that pretty much sums up our attitude to celebrity. We were at the VMAs and Rihanna was sitting in front of us. 'Louis!' I said, 'Look, there's Rihanna!' I was well impressed by that and we ended up chatting to her a bit. Don't get me wrong, we weren't suddenly best mates. You

don't see these people every day so you can't call them your friend, but if you're at the same awards 'do' one night, you end up chatting at some stage. Some awards ceremonies are better than others. The fan-voted awards are the best and we're so lucky 'cos our fans are ridiculous – the way they vote is nuts. The maddest awards are the ones where you beat the biggest artists in the world in the same category. That's always a shock.

Anyway, on this particular night at the VMAs all five of us lads were having a bit of a laugh, and we may have had the odd drink or two! Everyone was in these amazing ball-gowns and really fancy suits, all proper dressed up for the occasion. I can't even remember what we were wearing ourselves but we were all sitting there with these huge hot dogs covered in onions and mustard, trying to eat them without flicking sauce all over the place. Justin Timberlake got on stage and did this incredible performance, the crowd was going wild, there's wall to wall famous people looking amazing everywhere, but we're just trying to eat these hot dogs and have a laugh. At one point I noticed Louis just sniggering away, and then he leans over to me and says, 'Niall, we're hands down the worst celebrities on this planet!'

We were all really keen to get our third album out because we'd been so involved in the writing of that record. Before it came out, though, we had the small matter of releasing our own movie, *This Is Us*! That was just the best fun. The film crew had followed us on much of that big second album tour, starting off with footage of the multiple O2 shows we'd done. It was pretty mad having cameras around us for that long, but like I said before, we were 'born' on a TV show so we're used to having cameras around, at least when it's our own film crew. They don't really annoy you, they were just there ...

We were really excited about the film because Justin Bieber had done one, Katy Perry had done one and obviously way back the Spice Girls had made one too, so it seemed like a great idea. We tried to be as honest and open as we could for the film crew, and I think the movie is a pretty fair reflection of life in One Direction.

The première for the movie was the most ridiculous day. In fact I'd go so far as to say the London première might actually be the best day I've had in my career to date. Touring Australia and all the madness down there was big. The Verona show on tour when thousands and thousands of people showed up was memorable. The *Today* show, of course. MSG obviously ... Fortunately it's a long list of highlights but the film première is right up there.

First off it was the biggest crowd I've ever seen in Leicester Square. We'd been to a few premières before, *Harry Potter*, *Narnia*, all that, so we kind of knew what might happen, but I wasn't expecting the sheer numbers that were there that day. We stood on this platform and the size of the crowd was just ridiculous. I was like, 'Oh my God, I can't believe what I'm seeing!' It was one of those times when even in the middle of the red carpet we were looking at each other, in a small huddle, saying, 'Boys, what the hell is going on?!'

We went into the cinema and Simon Cowell was there, Ben Winston, Morgan Spurlock and various people from Sony and the film company, so we thanked them all. There was a room upstairs with a balcony looking out over Leicester Square, so we stood up there with Simon, he's in the corner with a fag in his mouth, we're drinking a few beers and before we knew it, me and Louis had had a few! Then Ronnie Wood came in. Ronnie Wood at our movie première for God's sake!

Me and Louis ended up sitting near the back with our families. Ben Winston's wife cheerily said, 'I couldn't hear a word of the film,' because me and Louis were messing like we were five years old, throwing Maltesers around, laughing at ourselves on the screen, literally like being at the back of class at school. I have a contagious laugh so when I start giggling everyone else starts laughing too, so mostly we spent the time sniggering and being frowned at.

All joking aside, though, that was a big moment. For me, it was the first time that I said, 'Crikey, lads, we must be quite famous. This is pretty cool.' Our own Leicester Square première, a red carpet with our name splattered all over it, huge screens everywhere, DJs, big star names coming out to see this with us. I loved every single second.

Promoting the third album on 23 November 2013 with 1D Day was a blast. Having our own TV show was immense but it took some doing, hosting that online show for seven hours! The team came up with some amazing ideas and guests, linking up with people in space, Robbie Williams, David Beckham – everyone was getting involved. In typical One Direction style, we were terrible at it. We pretty much blagged it, missing camera cues, fumbling our lines, making stuff up. It was hilarious, but somehow we got through it and people seemed to enjoy the whole day.

By then we were desperate to get our new album out and heard by our fans. Louis and Liam had over 20 songs written

It was pretty mad having cameras around us for that long, but like I said before, we were 'born' on a TV show so we're used to having cameras around, at least when it's our own film crew. They don't really annoy you, they were just there ...

EXPERIENCE THEIR LIVES ON THE RO **51**

1D | ONE DIRECTION

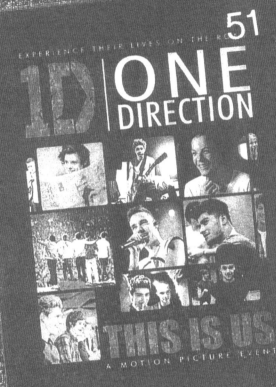

THIS IS US
A MOTION PICTURE EVENT

CREW

for that record, just through their pure dedication to the cause. It helped that by this point we had a team of song writers that we really liked and enjoyed working with, and everyone bounced around off each other really well.

We had always really wanted to get involved as much as we could with the songwriting for our albums, but we just had to wait till the time was right. We'd learned so much from the various producers and songwriters we'd been around on the first two albums, so I'd like to think we did a good job. The pressure was on to deliver a big album too, because now we had two huge-selling records behind us. I think that can only be a good thing because it pushes you on and gives you something to strive for.

When any new One Direction album is coming out, of course we get nervous because ultimately you don't know how it's going to go down. I always say to the lads, 'All we can do is try and make the record as strong as we can and then look for something good to happen.' Just before an album's release we get so anxious to put the record out there 'cos by then we've been living with those songs for months so we just want to get the fans' reactions.

Fortunately the fans seemed to like *Midnight Memories*. The commercial success of that record across so many countries was ridiculous, and hitting Number 1 in that many places was mad. I thought the success of *Up All Night* had tested my knowledge of geography but this was much more extreme! It meant so much to every single one of us in the band because of the personal nature of the album. We'd made such an effort to stamp our personalities and lives on these songs, so to see this collection of music be so well

received around the world was a massive deal for us. We were just delighted.

There was one challenge just around Christmas 2013 that could've threatened to derail the band's momentum – my serious knee injury. Back in the summer of *The X Factor* I was playing football on the green with my mates when I put my foot on the ball to drag it back when it suddenly felt like someone had kicked my knee out. I went flying up into the air and when I came back down my kneecap was hanging out. I went to a specialist and he said I had a floating kneecap. After that, the problem kept recurring. So for example, one time I was walking down Oxford Street and when I turned to dodge around someone my knee went again. I just ended up rolling around on the pavement right out in the street. Another time I was playing golf and I suddenly felt like I'd got an electric shock. In all it happened about eight times. Then I dislocated my knee on stage when me and Louis were messing about breakdancing one night. The lads were all trying to help me up off the ground but I was like, 'I can't move!' My face was white and my kneecap was just sticking out in the wrong place!

I'd started wearing a knee brace for support but it still wasn't right. It was clear that something needed to be done about the problem, especially now that it had impacted on my stage work. I had some MRIs, then I went to see this fella in the States called Dr Richard Steadman. He took one look at my leg and said, 'You have the knee of a 35-year-old footballer! I don't even have to look at your scans to tell you that you need an operation, big time.' Turns out my alignment was out too, so I really did need help!

I had a little time off for Christmas, then I went to the States on 4 January for an operation two days later. The surgeon performed a miracle – my knee is now fixed and in theory repaired forever. That said, I've a lot of strengthening work to do. When I got back I was lucky enough to be invited to do my rehab at the Chelsea training ground in Surrey. The daughter of José Mourinho (the team's manager) was a big One Direction fan and she'd previously come to our movie première. Next thing I know I get a text from José saying, 'I've heard about your knee, you're a good kid, absolutely no problem, come down here, use the facilities, the doctors, physios, whatever you need to get fit.'

So I started getting up at quarter past six in the morning to sit in traffic for two hours on the M25, on the way to my rehab at Chelsea's training ground. Before that you'd have struggled to get me out of bed before 1 or 2 in the afternoon. But I was on a mission to get fit for the stadium tour. I spent weeks going down there. At first I honestly assumed I'd be on the sidelines, but every single day I was in with the team. They gave me my own locker in the dressing room and my own kit with my initials on it, all laid out for me in the morning. The physio Steve Hughes looked after me during my seven weeks on crutches, cranking my leg to get it moving and literally teaching me to walk again. I worked with weighted suits, a treadmill in a swimming pool, all these high-tech gadgets. The bottom line is that without Chelsea's help there's no way I'd have made the tour in the shape I was in.

Every time I met José I was star-struck. Being around him is an incredible experience. He's so successful, yet he knew every person at that training ground by name and what they

I've had an amazing year! Thank you all sooo much! I'll never forget this tour!

did for Chelsea. One day he asked me, 'Niall, would you perhaps bring in some signed stuff for my daughter?' So I brought in some perfume, a T-shirt, and some bits and pieces. An hour later as I was leaving the training ground, he came running out and gave me this Chelsea bag with one of his training tops and a pair of his boots in it, signed for me. An absolute legend.

As I've said, the 2013 world tour was ridiculous. The scale of it was hard to take in, so you can imagine how we felt when it was put to us that there was a chance we could play stadiums on the next tour. We were all like, 'We won't sell out stadiums, forget that!' It's a big jump to go from theatres to arenas and there are plenty of bands who made that move too soon and paid the price. To then go from arenas – say 10–20,000 people – to stadiums filled with as many as 85,000 people is a massive gamble in a lot of ways. Don't get me wrong. We're confident of One Direction and we work hard to make the band succeed, but I'm not afraid to admit there was some trepidation when the idea of a stadium tour was first mentioned. We just said, 'Lads, surely there are much bigger artists out there who can't do stadiums, so why should we think One Direction can?'

In typical mad One Direction style, even announcing the stadium tour was nuts. We were working in Europe, then flew into London in the evening, went to Wembley the next morning and did the press conference to announce the tour. Then I think we flew straight back out to Europe for a gig that night! That reminds me. I keep meaning to check my Airmiles statement, I'm sure I should have quite a few by now!

We were all quite apprehensive when the first day of the ticket sales came around. We know we've a big fanbase and

We're having fun in tokyo!
konnichiwa!

FOR SOME REASON
LIVE TO THOUSAND
GIVES ME THIS AN
SECURITY, OF COM

ERFORMING
OF PEOPLE JUST
ZING FEELING OF
RT.

I LOVE
EVERY
SECOND.

we hoped the tour would sell well, but stadiums need to sell such a huge number of tickets. It's a big challenge. If you sold out a venue of 35,000 people most bands would be pretty pleased, but if you only sell that many for a Wembley Stadium show that's a relative failure.

So you can imagine how pleased we were when the ticket sales just blew up! First we heard that the Wembley Show had sold out in super-quick time, then they told us they'd put on another Wembley ... and then another Wembley. Same with Croke Park in Dublin – where I've been to see so many shows and matches – with multiple nights there to keep up with demand. It was just the best feeling. How lucky are we?

The first couple of weeks of any tour are always about getting used to the stage, the set, the whole performance. We rehearse hard, but you're never totally ready until you get out there in front of a crowd and perform. We always have a bit of a laugh with it too – we improvise, mess about, change parts of the show we don't enjoy. It can be a long year when you're out on the road for such an extended time, so switching it around and messing with the format can really help to keep you energised and fresh. That in turn just makes the gigs better for the fans, and that, after all, is the most important point.

I'm so lucky that I don't suffer from nerves when I get on stage (as I said earlier, I wish that was the case with TV appearances!). For some reason, performing live to thousands of people just gives me this amazing feeling of security, of comfort. I love every second. We love to have a bit of craic with the crowd and get them involved as much as we can. Once you know the show inside out it just becomes the best buzz every single night, and that's made all the more enjoyable because of our fantastic fans who really do bring out the best in all of us five lads.

You never come home from a One Direction show and say it was quiet. It's always unbelievably loud, the loudest show on the planet. We've actually done a decibel reading on it and measured 145 decibels in an arena – that's about the same level of noise as a NASA space shuttle taking off indoors. Honest to God.

I love it out there, and performing live is the best part of what we do. I do feel much more comfortable when I've got a guitar in my hand. I don't know why that is. I think it helps on stage generally too – everyone can be involved in the band. All the boys might come over to me, dance around, and the band can join in. It seems to create a sense of camaraderie.

When I think about how we're doing our own stadium tour around the world, it messes with my head. This is what I do this crazy job for – the thought of stepping out in front of tens of thousands of people every night gives me goosebumps. Unbelievable! Someone asked me just before the first show what I felt like and I said, 'I've never been so excited about anything in all my life.'

Being in One Direction has given me so much. The experiences I've had in this band are so incredible it's only when I sit back and work on something like this book that I can even begin to comprehend what an amazing time we've had. Hopefully people still enjoy watching us live and listening to our records, so maybe now, finally, I can see that those kids who came third in *The X Factor* have lasted more than six months. We've done all right, haven't we?

HOPEFULLY PEOPLE STILL ENJOY
WATCHING US LIVE AND LISTENING t
OUR RECORDS, SO MAYBE NOW, FINAL
I CAN SEE THAT THOSE KIDS WHO
CAME THIRD IN THE X FACTOR HAVE
LASTED MORE THAN SIX MONTHS.

WE'VE
DONE
ALL RIGHT,
HAVEN'T WE?

We were sitting at home one moment and then suddenly our lives changed forever, and here we are now. Maybe that's what people like about us. There's a sense of fun and a feeling that maybe in some way we're just normal lads who blagged it. Don't get me wrong, I'm not underestimating the hard work we've put in, the massive effort of our team and everyone involved in this band – there have been some serious amounts of work put in. Yet from day one we just wanted to be ourselves, have a great time, work hard and see where it took us.

No one knew this was going to happen. Even Simon Cowell is shocked at the scale of the band's success. You couldn't have ever predicted or imagined what's happened with One Direction in the last few years. I've been around the world with the lads and we have quite a few crazy times still ahead of us, no doubt. But do you know what? I'm still mad into this band.

Hav

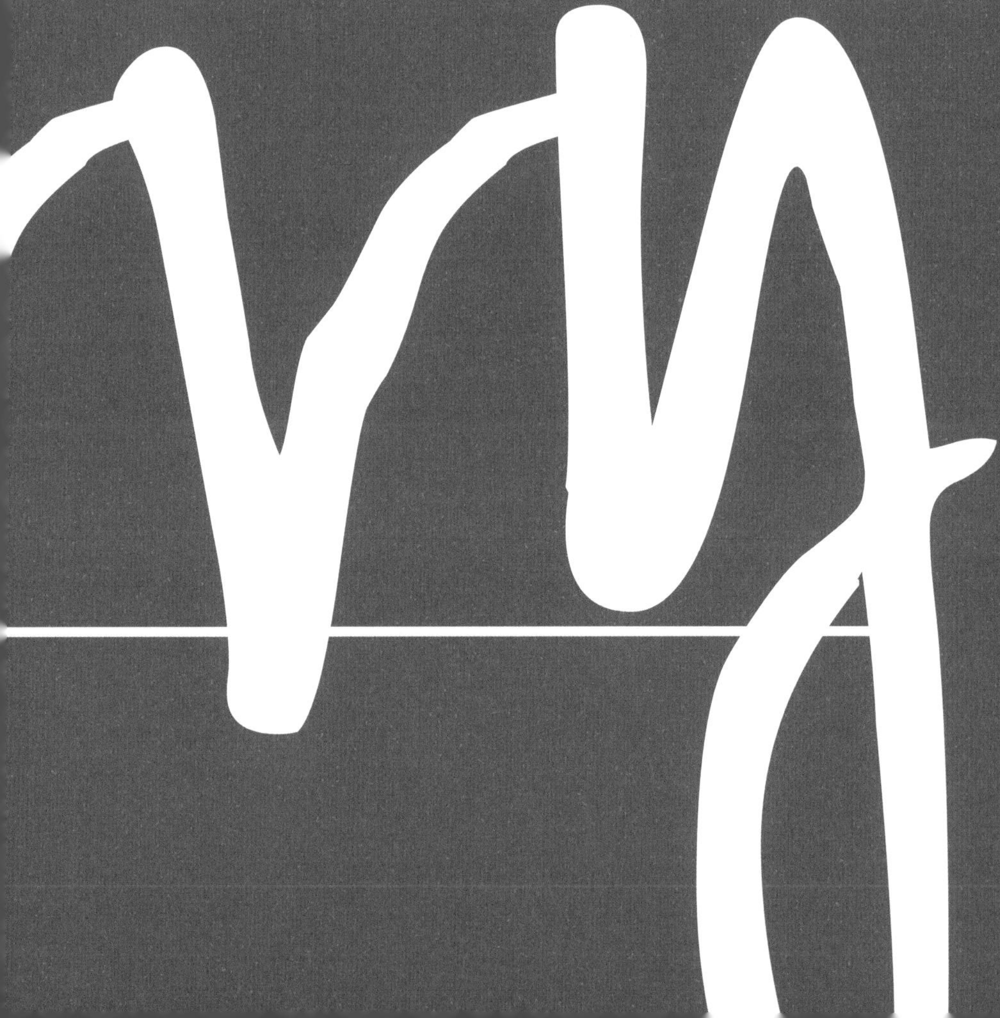

I guess my family would say I was a little bit of a show-off as a kid. From an early age my mum always thought I'd 'entertain' in some way. When I was at school I hadn't really decided exactly what it was I wanted to do, but I knew I really enjoyed performing and even at quite a young age got a real buzz from it. I think I was quite well behaved at school – well, maybe a bit cheeky with teachers but I don't think I was that naughty!

I always wanted to do well and definitely felt a sense of drive – maybe you could call it ambition, I don't know. I don't think I was necessarily that aware of the feeling at that point, it was just a sense that I wanted to succeed when I grew up. My parents were amazingly supportive – Mum would say, 'Harry, just get out there, have a go. If you don't even try how will you know if you could have done it? This is your dream we're talking about – we're behind you every step of the way.' They've always helped me try to achieve that.

In terms of my upbringing, I'm very lucky that my parents brought me up in the way that they did. I was always taught that everyone is equal, and it doesn't matter if you have a good job or not, or whether you earn a load of money or hardly any at all – it doesn't make a difference. My parents are incredible and support me in whatever I want to do. I'm not sure anything could have prepared me for what has happened in One Direction, but I do think those core values that my parents taught me have helped me to keep a sense of perspective on what has gone on. If I have kids some time in the future I'll absolutely want them to go and do better than me, as you'll always want the best for your kids. On top of that, I think any parent wants their kids to do something they

151

love. I'm incredibly fortunate that I get to do something that I love that just doesn't feel like a job.

I look back on the whole *X Factor* experience and I mainly think how incredibly young I was. It's hard to comprehend, really – I was literally just a kid. I'll always be so grateful for that programme and the opportunity it gave me. *The X Factor* has had such a huge impact on my life and I have no problem acknowledging the fact that I have that show to thank for being able to do what I do in this band. The show gave us that chance – yes, we took that opportunity and we've worked incredibly hard to make the most of it, but *The X Factor* just opened that door right at the beginning.

Because I was young and really quite inexperienced, I learned a huge amount in a short space of time. In some ways, *The X Factor* prepared us for life in One Direction. As we progressed in the show, a lot of people outside of the programme were saying we'd definitely get through each week and furthermore that we'd get a record deal for sure; all this stuff can feel like a lot of pressure and if you're not careful that can mess with your head. Luckily for us, there are a lot of great people involved with the show who kept us from getting carried away, allowed us to take our time and supported us through each week. They were really good at keeping us grounded. I remember one of the producers saying to us, 'Just take it one week at a time, don't listen to all the gossip you hear going on around you, keep working hard and stay focused.' Then as soon as we got off the show, it felt like there was even more hype. But by this point I felt like we were more prepared for that, and we knew to take things with a pinch of salt. With everything that has happened since those very early days on *The X Factor*, that measured start has always given us some perspective and a few tools to cope with the process. In terms of workload, the show is pretty intense too, so that also instilled a work ethic in us that would stand us in good stead.

The X Factor will always be a huge part of our life no matter whatever else we do, because that show started everything. It's not just the show itself either; I also have to thank everyone who was involved with it for giving me the opportunity – the judges, the crew, the producers, everyone. A lot of people believed in us and gave us that shot. Without them and their incredible hard work, we wouldn't be where we are today.

It's no secret that I was pretty emotional when we signed our record deal. In fact I was nervous more or less every time I went to see the record company; it can be quite an intimidating place when you're young – lots of grown-ups! I know it's a bit of a cliché, but being from a small town it was just so culturally different for me to walk into a big, swanky record-label office in the middle of London. Holmes Chapel is a small, very English town. Then suddenly I was hanging around these record-label offices and there were people from every corner of the world, people of all shapes and sizes. It was fantastic. Once you spend more time there, you realise all these people tend to be really creative and into the same kind of stuff as you – I found that instantly appealing. Still, to this day, I find people watching in London one of the best things to do. I love that. Back then, when I hadn't seen many people outside of my home town, it was just unreal. That's why the record-label offices always felt like being on a

Bottom: My big sister Gemma giving me hugs again!

Top: With my sister Gemma (far left) and our friends Sophie and Ryan Cantrill (second from left and far right).
Bottom: With my wonderful mum.

155

different planet. There was so much to take in and so many new perspectives, I remember it being really fun to be around and such an exciting and defining time for us.

The next step was to head off to Sweden and LA for the début album recording sessions. We were all pretty excited on the plane over. I was just shaking my head and said, 'I can't believe we are flying off to a recording studio!' and Niall was like, 'Sweden! We're going to record in Sweden. This is nuts!' None of us had a huge amount of experience of studios at all so this was another huge learning curve. I've since realised that that first trip to LA to record certain song parts was kind of crucial in terms of our first album and defining the band that we wanted to be – but to be honest, at the time I was just so excited to be there that I didn't really look at it in those terms. In fact, I distinctly remember waking up on the first morning in this amazing hotel and just thinking, *We're in Holly-woooood!* (That was the start of a special relationship I have with LA that I'll tell you more about a little later.) In retrospect I think that was a good way to be because I'd have felt too much pressure if I'd thought about things too much. I was just loving experiencing all these new people who were so creative and interesting – and really good fun!

Unlike *Midnight Memories* and to a lesser degree *Take Me Home*, we weren't involved much in the songwriting for the début album. Actually, I'm really glad we did it that way. It was a really good learning experience for us. If we'd gone in and tried to write an album ourselves it wouldn't have been good. We had no experience of doing ... well, anything really. We would've just been guessing at that point. We spoke about

Checking in with my family, catching up on sleep and eating too much – sounds like life on tour!

Harry

Looking at both of these photos, you can see I was a very happy kid, for which I feel very fortunate.

this together as a band at the time. One night I said, 'There's no way I'm going to start telling these guys how I think we should sing!' Louis was pretty quiet, and Zayn said, 'I have all these ideas buzzing around in my head, but I know we need to listen to what they're saying.' We all recognised these guys knew exactly what they were doing.

The producers were brilliant and they knew that this was the best way to get an amazing début album for One Direction. When you go in at such a young age and you're working with a songwriter and a producer who've done all these amazing songs and you haven't done *anything* in a studio, you certainly don't feel comfortable to say, 'What if I sing it like this instead?' You don't wanna tell someone who has had a million Number 1s how a song should be done. It was important for us to listen and learn, to do what was being asked of us and then later on take those lessons and try and adapt from there, rather than just jumping into the deep end and trying to write songs too early.

When we flew back into the UK we had a big shock to see so many of our amazing fans at the airport. That was a major moment for One Direction. I remember as we were heading into the airport, someone said to us that loads of fans were waiting there, but their words, 'I think there are quite a lot of people!' didn't really prepare us! When I first turned a corner in the airport and saw the crowds, I said, 'Oh my God, lads, you're not going to believe what I'm looking at!' It really was chaos, there were so many fans. Eventually we were escorted away and holed up in this valet parking office somewhere in the terminal, then bundled into a proper police riot van. When the doors shut on that van, we all just looked around at each other completely dazed, took a minute and then we were like, 'That was intense!' That's exactly the right word. It was the most intense experience we'd had so far.

Mentally, that was a big deal for us. We'd met quite a few fans out in Sweden at the studio sessions, which had taken us aback, especially as that was in another country. But Heathrow was on another level altogether. Not so much in terms of the publicity or attention we received – it was simply the most intense experience we'd had so far. I remember it having a big impact on all five of us and our team. The fans were shouting our names, singing the lyrics to our songs, calling out, 'We love you!' They were just amazing.

Back when we did the early PA shows and first book signings these were publicised events, and naturally we'd be surprised at just how many people would show up. So to have that many people take time out of their day and go all the way to Heathrow was just nuts. It's something I'll never be able to thank the fans for enough.

By the time our début single was ready for release, I felt a sense of responsibility that this song was what we could give back to the fans who had done so much for us across social media, had come down to recording studios and supported us so strongly throughout and then after *The X Factor*. I felt as if we had to earn their support. I still do.

The early nerves were still very much there when we heard 'What Makes You Beautiful' on the radio for the first time. I remember we went into Radio 1 and we were all just so excited. Scott Mills was really supportive, and just as he pressed Play on the song he said, 'Please like it!' Then as the tune started, we were all just shaking our heads. Louis said,

thanks for having us, Raleigh, NC. you were very, very loud. X

WE KNOW HOW MUCH
ENERGY PEOPLE HAVE
PUT IN — AND STILL
DO — TO THIS BAND.

THAT'S

NEVER

UNDERESTIMATED.

'This is unreal,' and had his hands on his head, and I was jumping up and down singing along. What a buzz! Then on the way home from the station they played it again, while we were in the car. We all really liked the song but when you're putting it out there you feel so vulnerable; it just feels like you're putting *yourself* out there to be criticised. It was definitely a nervous time for us and we were just so happy that people liked it. To get a Number 1 was insane, beyond our wildest expectations. I remember when our management told us we had hit the top spot I was just shaking my head and going, 'This is crazy!' And it wasn't just the girls who liked us. There were even a few guys out there saying they loved the song.

Like I said about Sweden, we were still getting used to fans in the UK so when we had to do the 'Bring 1D To Me' campaign – which took in four European countries in four days – it seemed completely surreal. I remember saying to the lads, 'How do these people even know about us?' I actually thought to myself, *Why are we even going to Europe?* We didn't really get it, but what was happening was that the word of mouth and social media buzz around the band was travelling so fast it was almost out of control.

As a band, we're really lucky that we live in a time like this, when social media can let so many people know about our music so quickly. Compared with how the music industry worked 50, 20, even five years ago, the impact of social media has been enormous. We were fortunate to arrive just as this was beginning to be felt. I have to say, though, social media doesn't create itself. We had this army of fans out there on Twitter and Facebook, just constantly posting stuff,

164

MeXICoooo

and the speed and scale of how they networked news about One Direction out there was ridiculous. We're so grateful for that. We know how much energy people have put in – and still do – to this band. That's *never* underestimated.

The exciting news kept on coming. It really was just this blur of work and crazy stuff going on. By the time of the début album, we knew that we had an amazing fanbase and so we had strong hopes for the record. But to see it hit Number 2 in the UK and even go one higher in so many other countries was hard to comprehend, to be honest with you. I was a 17-year-old kid. I kinda couldn't get my head around it at the time 'cos it didn't really sit with me. It still hasn't, if I'm being totally straight with you. We've always wanted to keep things moving and have been ambitious in driving for the next thing, so it kinda happened and we could briefly recognise how amazing that was, but then we didn't really have time to let the achievement settle in. We just had to keep moving. So it was kinda like we knew it was incredible and amazing, but we never felt we had time to sit and say to each other, 'Jeez, we're Number 1!' It was more a case of, 'Lads, see you at 5am in the bus. We've got a radio interview first, then a photo shoot, then …'

When I look back at that period now, I can't believe I was only 17 at the time. I also find it really strange to think that so much time has passed since then. It feels young to be 20, so looking back to when I was 17 and remembering all of that stuff happening is mad. The whole thing is outrageous. I recognise that it was outrageous then and that it still is now. It's a hard thing to describe. I wanna write these really clever and concise words that sum up the whole crazy experience

166

...we started to believe that maybe we, as a band, could genuinely take off.

and my emotions at the time, but it's so difficult, so strange, so amazing ... You can never really put into words how it makes you feel.

What I *can* say is that 2011 was such a great year. We'd done those really early PA shows, then the *X Factor* tour, promo and interviews, radio station visits, and then the single had hit Number 1, the album Number 2. It was just a crazy period when we started to believe that maybe we, as a band, could genuinely take off. Even so, by the time we got to the December tour we were still pretty nervous. People probably assume that we just think everything is going to go to plan and be a huge success, but that's not the case. We had nerves then and we still have them now. We really focus on every show and get nervous every time we put ourselves out there again. You can never let your guard down because the fans deserve the very best.

So the UK début album tour felt like high stakes to me. Our own headline shows, bigger venues ... I was feeling the pressure. We still kinda felt like we were blagging it a lot. That tour was a step up – it felt like it was the first thing we were doing on our own and it was big. So we all felt the same. We were like, 'There's absolutely no way we can allow any of this tour to be bad. It just can't be allowed to fail.' It felt like that tour was a lot about inviting people to experience with us the fun we had on a daily basis. Fortunately, the show went down really well and we felt like we'd done the fans proud – that it wasn't just a load of hype, that they'd had just as much fun as we'd had on stage.

Talking of proving ourselves, we flew out to the States in February 2012 with very modest expectations. We had just about got used to the idea that fans across Europe knew about One Direction, although that had been a bit of a shock. But we were pretty sure that not many kids out in the States would have a clue who we were. I said to the lads, 'I'm just excited to be going out there. I'm keen to see what the US is like.'

I think anyone from England is usually pretty excited when they first go to America. The nearest I'd had to that feeling was going to London for *The X Factor*. The capital seemed such a long way from home, geographically and culturally. It was just so different to the way I was used to living. I'd thought I wouldn't go to London till I was maybe 30, so that first trip down there was a big deal for me. Well, America is like that, but *tenfold*. I loved the pure excitement of being somewhere that's filled with things you've only seen in movies and on TV. Still do.

It's often the case that if someone is big in the US they're automatically big in Britain, but going the other way across is not so simple. I felt very aware that it was a good time for British acts in America. Adele had completely opened up a gateway out there, which definitely helped, as well as people like Ed Sheeran, Mumford & Sons, acts like that, who've all created an atmosphere that's really receptive to British music. I've no doubt that we got very lucky with the timing of things.

Of course, our amazing fans had already done so much groundwork for us too. The fact that you can have a direct conversation – genuine, direct contact – with someone who you watch on the TV is just an amazing thing. With the States in particular, prior to social media being this big, if you were gonna have a profile over there it would probably involve years and years of massive tours, relentless promo, a real hard slog physically working your way across the country. But in this generation bands can communicate through so many different mediums. It's an amazing time to be around in that respect, for sure.

We quickly realised there was a good deal of interest in the band from the number of interviews we were doing. Then they eventually had to bring the album release forward a week due to the level of interest. 'What Makes You Beautiful' went Top 30 and that ramped it up another level too. We did a signing in a shopping mall and that was just nuts. It was the first one we'd done over there and we didn't think it'd be that big – even 100 kids would have blown us away – but again those incredible fans supported us in their thousands. Just incredible!

The momentum seemed to snowball from there. The support slot touring with Big Time Rush was a huge plus for us so early on in the States. On the first night I saw someone wearing a One Direction T-shirt and I was like, 'Lads, that's a bit weird!' Then these fans knew all the words to every song. Even if we didn't dare to believe it, we could kind of feel it.

We finished the tour and had the album coming out soon. Appearing on the *Today* show was the first massive moment for us in the US. We'd been told it was a prestigious thing to be asked to perform – being a Brit I wasn't familiar with the show but when we saw the thousands of fans who turned up it was just breathtaking. Some of the streets in New York are so narrow and they were literally filled with this sea of people. To us it just seemed like everywhere you looked there were skyscrapers towering over this mass of faces. There were

YOU CAN NEVER LET
YOUR GUARD DOWN
BECAUSE THE FANS
DESERVE THE

VERY

BEST?!

even people hanging out of the windows of the skyscrapers – it was amazing. At the start of our performance when I shouted, 'New York City, make some noise!' the whole place just went completely nuts. What an experience!

Even now, every time we do anything overseas we're still so surprised by the response. I know people probably think that's rubbish, because One Direction have had a good amount of international success, but it's true. I personally still find it a shock when we go abroad and there are thousands of people waiting for us or coming to our shows. It's still not what I expect when we're in a different country. Back then you could magnify that feeling a thousand times. We definitely didn't expect it from somewhere like the US. So you can imagine what an experience the *Today* show was. Everything about that performance ... there wasn't one part of that day that wasn't amazing. That was the first time I'd been to New York as well!

The momentum just kept building and building. During that period, we were playing a show in Nashville and Steve Barnett, who ran our US record label at the time, came into the dressing room and he was like, 'We think you might get a Number 1 album.' We were like, 'What?!' We'd heard a few conversations when it was discussed but really, to us, that was just talk. People say stuff like that all the time to encourage you and keep things positive. The actual thought of being Number 1 in the States with our début album just seemed totally incomprehensible. No other British act had ever done that, so why us?

Then Steve said, 'It's close, lads. You might miss it, but if you really want that Number 1 you're gonna have to work

I got tied up.

Harry

harder than you've ever done before.' There was no question for us. From that moment we worked as hard as we possibly could. We did signings in lunch breaks, promo all over the place, every spare second was used finding another way to push the album. We'd got a chance for that Number 1 and we just went for it.

I knew it would be a big deal if we did top the charts, but I didn't know how big a deal it was until later on. I don't think I really took in the scale of our achievement for a while afterwards. It just didn't hit me what the true significance was. We were so busy promoting and doing shows, all that, so it was hard to associate what we'd achieved with all this talk of other massive British bands who'd done the same. We were so young, we weren't about to sit back and think about all this history, all this context. Besides, we didn't have the time. It was amazing, though. It felt like everything we'd done previously was leading up to that point. Just after we all found out, I said to the lads, 'Getting that Number 1 is a big turning point for us. It's a big moment.'

In One Direction we've always been very proud of the live shows we put on – it's our chance to perform our records to these amazing fans who've put us in the position that we're in. In a way, we kinda did the process in reverse, certainly in the US anyway. Traditionally, bands would go over there and tour really hard, then put the album out and hope to sell it to people in that way. For us, the tour felt like such a celebration of the success of our album and an opportunity to say thank you. It felt like we'd worked so hard to get there and now we could just have fun every night with all the people who had supported us.

We went to Australia on tour too, which was completely nuts. Those dates were insane to me 'cos it was just crazy to think there were people from the other side of the world who even knew who we were. To be such a long way from home and have that support always feels very special to me.

We were doing quite a bit of promo, but we were having such a great time, so to us we didn't really see what was happening with the band's profile. We were still just taking each day, one at a time. There was so much work and travelling – I guess it's hard to necessarily see the big picture when you are involved as you have no peripheral vision. I was like, 'Let's just keep our heads down working hard and try to put on our very best show every night.' You don't realise everything that's happening. I try to take a step back as often as I'm able, 'cos I think it's important to do that so you can appreciate exactly what's going on. Ultimately, though, I think there's no way any of us five can really get a proper grasp of what it's like to see One Direction from the outside.

As much as the US was incredibly exciting, it's always brilliant to get home and perform for the UK fans. The best example of that during this period was playing at the closing ceremony of the London Olympics. I think the rest of the lads will probably be the same as me – I actually don't remember much about that day because it was a bit of a blur, to be honest! We were in and out of the stadium so fast. I do remember the huge number of people in there, it was insane. It was crazy to think of something that was so big for London and the UK, and that we were involved in it. People kept asking me what it felt like and all I could say was, 'I feel really proud. That's the biggest emotion, just an overwhelming sense of pride.' It was a huge moment for the country and the opportunity to be a part of that in any way was amazing. It didn't make us any less nervous that we only had to sing half of one song, but it was cool. We were completely shocked by the sort of names that we were surrounded by, the level of artists that we were among was ridiculous. Plus, we were singing on a truck, so I remember being pretty focused, I said to the lads at one point, 'Just make sure none of us fall off!'

I couldn't possibly reflect on this period without mentioning Madison Square Garden. I know we've talked about this before but it really was just the most incredible day. The actual show felt like a step up for us. MSG was really a night when we all pushed ourselves to the limit – we found another gear. I think that extra energy came naturally from the history of the venue as well. You walk down the hallway and see all these photos, and somehow it gets into your head and makes your performance better. I was walking along a corridor with Liam at one point and we were both looking at all these famous faces, and I said, 'Jeez, this place is amazing. You can literally feel the history.' His dad's the same as mine, really into his music, so he was like, 'Dad would love to see all of this!'

What was also particularly special, apart from the gig itself and the crazy history of the place, was the party afterwards, because we were able to invite pretty much everyone who'd ever worked with the band – people from the record label, management, crew, marketing. We all just hung out and had a party afterwards. The whole lot of us had worked so hard, this was the end of an amazing campaign and that party was a brilliant way to celebrate everyone's success.

MSG

A couple of months before the Olympics, in the spring of 2012, we'd started writing for the second album and, to be honest, that feeling of being on a cloud, that sense of unreality, was still there. We started writing for the second record on the road and, despite the first album doing well in so many countries, I didn't feel like there was a great deal of pressure. Or should I say, the band didn't seem to show they were under any pressure. I was personally just so looking forward to getting into the studio and, hopefully, contributing more to the songwriting of the record this time. So there was very little apprehension – it was more a feeling of excitement. We were having fun and hoping that people continued to like us. It seemed to work, so we just kept going that way.

I can see that our approach was pretty naïve but I don't think that's necessarily a bad thing. We were just really focused on making a great record. You don't consciously go into the studio and say, 'We're going to write a Number 1 album!' That's just not possible or desirable. Plus, you write each song on its own, so you're collating this collection of individual songs, just trying to make each one as good as it can be. Once again, we weren't over-thinking it. We didn't deliberately take a more relaxed approach. Thankfully people seemed to like that.

I felt the expectation around the second album more during the actual week of release. By then you just want people to hear the record and say they think it's wicked. You want to hear their opinions. Then in the few days before you get the chart position, it's only natural to want to see where it will land. How can you not be keen to know? Maybe then you start thinking about the Number 1.

One Direction have a habit of delivering the most amazing news at the most ordinary moment. I knew our second album was doing really well in the States on its week of release and there was a very good chance we might even go in at Number 1 again. That week I'd a few days off after we'd just finished a New York trip and had stayed on for a few extra days, just exploring the city. I'd been on a bike ride and was returning the bike I'd rented to the shop, when I got a call saying, 'Harry, the album's Number 1.' I was completely on my own in this bike shop, I had my hands full, my phone was perched on my shoulder up to my ear, I was talking to this guy trying to give him the bike back and at the same time having a conversation about being Number 1 in the States. I was like, 'Really? That's wicked!' I got off the phone, sorted the bike thing out and went outside, and I was like, *Hang on a minute. We're Number 1 again!* I had pizza to celebrate. *Up All Night* had done so well, and we knew it had set a tough target to beat. To know that *Take Me Home* had exceeded that success was a lot to comprehend.

I don't think we'll ever 'get used' to chart success and everything that goes on around us. We just all look at each other and go, 'This is brilliant, lads!' Let's be completely honest here – we still kinda felt like we were blagging it a bit. Yes, we'd put in the graft but there's always a sense of, 'We don't know why this is happening, but let's work more and more and more, and maybe it will keep happening.' It felt amazing. Honestly, that was our reaction. We didn't really know what to do with it, in a way, so we just kept working.

We did some great gigs around this point, one of which was the Royal Variety Show in front of the Queen. It's an institution in the UK and, of course, anything involving the Queen makes you feel you need to have your best suit on. She's one of those people who you think you're never going to get anywhere near. So the fact that we were going to perform in front of her and then meet her felt a bit outrageous. I remember not wanting to mess it up, but that's the kind of feeling that has got me through most things – just don't mess up.

I think this is a good point in the book to talk to you about the pretty serious confidence issues I suffered as a result of an early problem I had on stage. As many of you know, we appeared on a big Saturday night TV show in the UK and I wasn't happy at all with my vocal. After the performance I saw some comments online that I struggled with. In the documentary we made during this time there's a well-known piece to camera where I explained why that incident upset me so much, and I think what I said is pretty self-explanatory.

However, what I didn't know then was that ultimately that experience would turn into a positive – it became a great learning curve for me. Yes, at the time I was gutted and those comments online really upset me, genuinely. I'll be totally honest here and say that it all played on my mind for a long time. Part of the issue was that we had done loads of TV shows so much better. This was easily the worst I had done, so that was frustrating, but it was the only performance people talked about for a while. I'm naturally a fairly confident person – in most situations, but not all. That whole episode was a big knock to my confidence for quite some time.

I now know why it happened. At that point any natural confidence I had in myself was just being taken over by nerves,

THE
ROYAL
VARIETY
PERFORMANCE

2012

ARTIST

17th – 19th November 2012

I remember not wanting to mess it up - but that's the kind of feeling that has got me through most things —

just
don't
mess
up.

because I'd no idea back then how to channel and control my anxiety. Sometimes just standing on a stage used to make me nervous. However, One Direction have always been a band that gigs heavily and promotes the music with TV and radio appearances where we perform live. So, over time I've been able to learn about nerves, to understand why and when they might hit, and best of all how to control them. Now it's a totally different ball game. That early bad TV experience taught me that I had to control my nerves if I was to sing well. In fact, I know now that if your nerves are controlled correctly they can actually give you a bit of an edge, an extra sense of focus. If you let them completely take over they can really put you off. It's easy for me to look back now and take the positives, perhaps, and I certainly remember how upset I felt at the time, but I do have this view on life that you need to be positive. When something difficult happens to you, take a step back and look at what possible positives might come out of it. I was lucky to have had that experience and I feel I'm a better performer for having learned the lessons I did from it.

I think the tight-knit nature of the band kept our feet on the ground through these early phases. There were also a few specific experiences that you'd have to be inhuman not to be affected by. One in particular was when we went to Ghana in aid of Comic Relief.

You see so many of those fund-raising shows on telly, with footage of sadly very poverty-stricken places, and it always affects you, of course. Sometimes you kinda think things like, *How bad can it really be?* You can't fully comprehend the severity and the sheer physicality until you actually see,

If you want a
job doing proper
...Do it yourself.

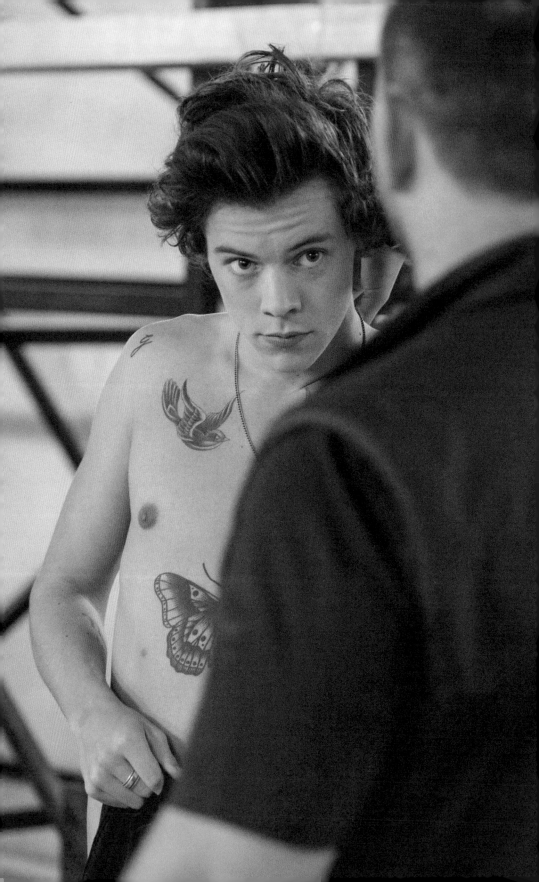

hear, smell, touch and taste it yourself. When you go to places where people are living in abject poverty, your senses are just completely bombarded, overwhelmed. The smell is so intense, the smoke hurts your eyes, you can really see how dirty these places are, with so many strange sounds, and everything you touch seems dirty. You go and visit these lovely, amazing people who are living in extreme hardship with such dignity, and you literally cannot believe what you're seeing. I remember saying to Liam at one point, 'Can you imagine living here all the time? We're going back to our hotels tonight, warm shower, food, all that, but these people are always here …'

That trip really hit me hard. It did with all of us. There are no words to express the mixture of emotions. It was the ultimate sense of perspective, such a massive contrast to what was going on with One Direction at the time. How can you go to somewhere like that and not come away thinking, *Any problem I have is relative, nothing I have to put up with is anywhere near that*? Of course, people who are not in poverty can have serious problems too – everything is relative – but when people living in the West have difficulties it can really mask their judgement and they can get a really smoky mind about what real problems are. I'll never, ever forget what I saw and what it represents.

I think in life it's important that you have experiences like that. With the position that we're in with the band, we're lucky enough to see things like that and learn from them. I think it's important that you try to make a difference, even if it's only a small difference. You simply cannot live and think that problems like these don't exist. It's naïve, and you're deluded if

189

you try to block it out and think it's not your problem. It *is* your problem. At the end of the day we all have to do what we can to help.

Once we'd got back from Ghana we hit the road again with a new sense of perspective. The number of shows was huge and the actual arenas themselves were massive. We were going to places that we'd played before, but back then we'd just be doing say three songs with maybe five other acts on a big multiple band line-up. This time around it was our headline gig and the shows were sell-outs. For most of that tour we were just surprised to have a band opening for us, rather than us opening for someone else. It was just crazy and it seemed a bit unreal.

One aspect of being on the road that I absolutely love is the chance to travel and see so many places. When I step back from and reflect on what my job allows me to do (if I can call it a job), I realise I'm amazingly lucky. I get to meet so many interesting people and see so many parts of the world. Travelling is something that I always wanted to do, and although I might be doing it a little bit differently to walking around with a backpack on my shoulders, it's still travelling. You still get to see amazing places. I get to do all this cool stuff that when I was 16 I never thought would happen.

It's always fun going exploring. Usually when I get to places I haven't been to before, I try to meet someone or a family who lives there and just let them show me round. That's usually how I feel I can get the best experience. One time I was in Chicago and someone put me in touch with a local guy who was happy to show me round. We played golf, and then I went back to his house for a barbecue with his family and kids.

Of course, you wouldn't be human if you didn't miss home sometimes on the road. We do so much travelling that I've learned to not become too attached to any one particular place. I don't see the point of becoming settled in one area just yet, because it's a fact that at the moment I'll not be there very often or for very long. That impacts on your private life because you find yourself making arrangements for six months time that you have every intention of keeping, but then something happens with the band and you end up in a completely different part of the world and can't make it.

When you haven't really been back home properly for four years, that's quite tough. Missing my family is probably the worst part of being in One Direction, but I'm also very lucky because they're so supportive. I couldn't ask for a better family. Mum and Dad will have so many questions – 'How have you been? Where are you at the moment? What's hap-pening tomorrow?' The usual stuff parents ask when they haven't seen you for a while. They just want to know that I'm OK. It's really lovely. They know that sometimes I'm really busy and can't talk straight away, but when I can they're always there to chat.

Sometimes you just have to see things in a different way, though. It would be easy to moan about being away from family, or penned up in a hotel and not being able to go out to sightsee as much as you'd like. But that's too negative. OK, you can't necessarily just go out into a city and do tourist stuff whenever you like, but at the same time you might not even be in that country in the first place if it wasn't for the

191

band. Most of the time I do get to see these places and I feel very fortunate.

My love of travel has led me to buy a place in Los Angeles. That city is somewhere I feel good being in. There's something about the sunshine – I know that's probably a bit of a cliché, but I like it. There's something about waking up to sun, that feeling of just wanting to be outside; the great weather makes me want to do stuff. If I wake up and it's grey I wanna stay in bed! In LA you get to be outside when you have breakfast, lunch and dinner. Even if my car breaks down, I'll just stand in the sun for an hour and wait for the tow truck!

I also have good friends there. You do hear a lot of horror stories in the music business from that city but, in my opinion, LA completely depends on who you you hang out with. If you surround yourself with people who are into all that superficial stuff, then you become superficial yourself. However, if you instead surround yourself with good, normal people, you'll be fine. You need friends there. I'm lucky to have that so I really enjoy my time over there.

We did learn quite quickly that not everything you read about 'relationships' in the newspapers is necessarily true. However, following on from that, because this band is in the public eye, I'm also aware and accepting of the fact that if one of us has a new relationship then it may be of interest to people who follow the band. I get all that. Gossip is natural.

I can totally see why our relationships might attract attention and interest, given that we're in a well-known band. I don't necessarily believe it's of particular interest myself, but I can see why some people might be interested. Obviously if

you guys look amazing
@todayshow

I'm with someone who's in the public eye, of course, that increases public and media interest. To a degree, all that comes with the job. I get that. What I would say is that some of the relationships that got reported were when I was in my late teens, so I was learning along the way just like every kid of that age. I love meeting interesting people and I enjoy having a relationship with a girl if I think she's really special. I don't think I'm unusual in that. I know that I won't necessarily always be allowed the luxury of total privacy, because of being in the band, and I'm not about to complain about that, not least because doing my job gives me so many amazing benefits. Hopefully people will just see that I'm trying to find my way like every one else of my age and I'm no different in that respect.

Having said that, it's quite funny sometimes when you get 'linked' with people you might've only met once, or sometimes not at all! More so when the band first started, I'd go out with a mate and his girlfriend and if we were seen out I'd suddenly be 'linked' to this person I'd probably only met that night! I take it with a pinch of salt, to be fair. It doesn't really worry me and I genuinely do understand why it provokes interest. I might not agree all the time, but I do get where it comes from.

I think the fairest and most honest response from me regarding any tag I seem to have been given about relationships is to suggest that if you put any 16-year-old boy who's obviously interested in girls into the position I found myself in at that age, then it kind of might go that way a little bit!

On a related note, I can definitely see how being in the public eye could change someone. I think that's why I've always made myself take a step back, to kind of just see it as what it is, so that it doesn't become normal life. If you think that life in a pop band is normal, that it's normal for you to stand on stage and sing to 50,000 people, that it's normal for girls to wait outside your hotel all day and night just to say 'Hello' for two minutes ... if you ever think all that's normal, well, then you're in trouble. That's not normal, in any way.

I think it's very important that your mindset keeps hold of that crucial fact because otherwise it can become your whole life. I always try to retain some element of a private life, so I go and work with the band really hard and then when I'm not working I like to just see friends and hang out, go swimming, have a meal out, or whatever. After a gig or a really hard day with the band I always need an hour or so to unwind a little bit. It's an amazing life to have, but I think the reason why people sometimes struggle with it is because the lines can very easily become blurred. It's a tricky balance to maintain.

For example, seeing the stage for our 2014 stadium tour for the first time completely took my breath away. As I walked round the corner from backstage and the full scale of the set hit me, I just said, 'Oh my God!' out loud. We were all stunned. In fact, I reacted in exactly the same way as I did to certain big moments at the very start of One Direction, so I'm really pleased to still be able to get such an intense buzz. There are still surprises that I can be completely taken aback by. It hasn't become normal to me, at all. I hope it never will.

It's obviously odd when people talk about us being famous. We all feel that way. I know we're recognised but none of us considers ourselves 'famous' in that respect. Perhaps that's helped us take so much in our stride, because we just still

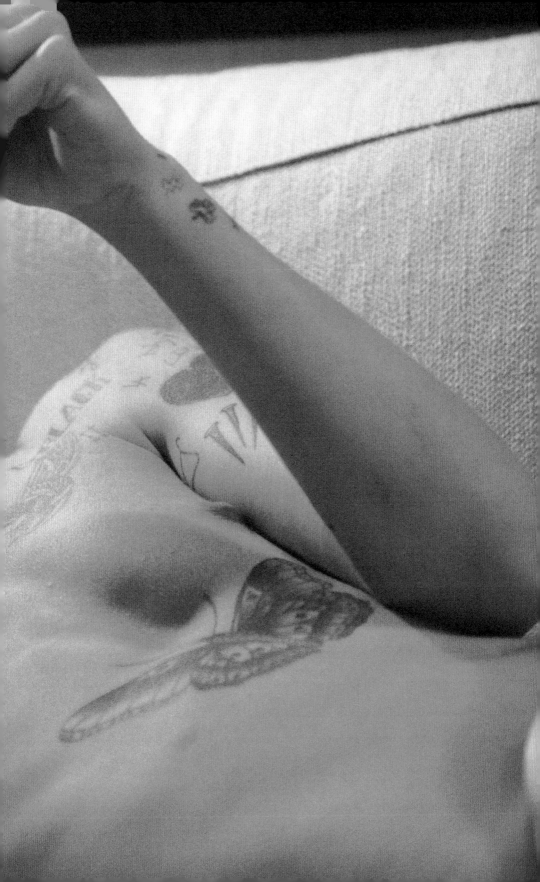

I think it
important
you try
a differe
if it's on
small diff

s

that

o make

ce, even

a

rence.

feel outsiders, in a way. There's times when I'll be sat at dinner with a famous person who's there perhaps as a friend of a friend, and I'm chatting away having a nice time and then suddenly I think, *Oh my God, that's so-and-so!* Then I feel about 14 years old. If they're talking to me and say 'Harry', it freaks me out.

I feel very lucky that being in One Direction enables me to meet certain people that I've been a fan of since I was a kid. There have been so many famous people that we've been lucky to meet and I'm not gonna mention them all here, but certain ones do stand out. Take Martin Scorsese, for example. He came to meet us backstage at Madison Square Garden and that was just the most surreal moment. When you meet a name that's just so big, a proper household name who everybody recognises as a genius, it's an odd feeling. You know you're really in the presence of a person who's changed stuff, who's really made a difference to the way things are done.

If I meet those kind of people I tend to be completely in awe of them. I'm star-struck. Conversely, I know that some people might feel 'star-struck' when they meet the band. That's daft to us, but we do see some fans getting pretty intense. Then I start to wonder, *Is that how people see me? As famous?* We're just people and our job means we happen to be in a high-profile position. Other than that, how are we any different to anyone else? Same goes for Martin Scorsese and all the famous people I've met. They're just people at the end of the day.

The funny thing is, I hate the word 'fame' because I don't think it should define someone. You often hear people say,

'This is when he was famous and then after that he wasn't as famous,' which seems to mean that the person is a failure now because he's not as famous as he once was. It's like a timeline. People seem to use the period when someone was famous as a barometer of failure. In that sense I don't like the word.

I've noticed I really enjoy meeting famous people who my parents are fans of! Somehow this makes the experience even more special, and I love telling Mum and Dad about it, or better still getting them to meet that person too. It excites me to see how much it excites them. I was talking to my dad about Rod Stewart one time, and Dad was telling me about a gig years ago when he climbed up on to these rugby posts to get a glimpse of Rod. I love it when things like that happen.

I'm always looking to learn from people who are more experienced than me. I feel like I can learn a lot from the 'famous' people I occasionally meet because many of these big stars are so grounded. It makes me think that it can be done – you *can* be involved in a successful band and be in the public eye, and not become a bit of a diva. Also, it makes me realise that people are just people. It's like I was saying at the start of this chapter about my parents teaching me that everyone's equal. I certainly don't think having a high profile makes me better than anyone else. If you make an effort you can find common ground with everyone.

Events around our third album *Midnight Memories* were just completely crazy. Making the movie *This Is Us* was an amazing experience. We're used to the cameras, so that was pretty fun and just seeing so many people enjoy our film was amazing. Leicester Square – well, what can you say about

Harry interviewing fans at the #ldmoviepremiere!

that?! What a day! I think that was one of the few occasions when we were all able to acknowledge that maybe the band was pretty big, that maybe it has gone pretty well. It was a rare moment to step back and see how far we'd come. It was so enjoyable. Same with 1D Day. How can you not enjoy being supported by so many people for that many hours in one day? It was really enjoyable having that direct link again too. This is the most exciting part of using the new social media and technology – you can foster that relationship and keep it cared for. The fans deserve to be looked after. We're so lucky with our fans, we have to pinch ourselves sometimes.

The anticipation for the tour is immense. When we first saw the stage at tour rehearsals we were all overwhelmed. The opportunity to perform in front of so many fans in so many countries is such a privilege. The selfish part of me also can't wait to get that buzz you experience from performing live. The adrenalin you get is said to be like a drug and I'd certainly say that it could be addictive. If I was to leave the environment where I perform in front of a crowd, there's no doubt that I'd miss the adrenalin hugely. I think it's the best time you can have. There's such a pure, unadulterated sense of enjoyment, a buzz, a wave of excitement, it's just the best feeling ever. To have the opportunity to do that all over the world again is something we're all very grateful for.

I feel like One Direction is a one in a million opportunity for us. It certainly doesn't happen very often, and in some ways it's been a unique thing to have to learn to understand. They don't give out lessons on how to deal with all of this. Yes, it's

completely crazy at times, but there are five of us who know exactly what the other people in this band are feeling. That's always a very cool part of being in this band. I feel like whatever happens in the future and however things go, we'll always have it in common that we went through this together. All of the stuff that's happened to One Direction, if you think about it, is mind-blowing.

A lot of people will say to you that life is short. That's easy to dismiss as a cliché, but what I've learned along the way is that life *is* so short – so you might as well enjoy it as much as you can.

In the general gist of things, so many people want to be famous and crave the attention that accompanies fame, but as soon as they get it they're like, *Oh! This isn't always nice.* But you really have to think to yourself, *There's not one part of this that you can complain about and think isn't worth it. The pros will always outweigh the cons.*

I'm extremely grateful for the opportunities this band has given me. There are certainly jobs that are very demanding and often badly rewarded. By comparison, I really don't have much to moan about. I'm incredibly fortunate that I've had this opportunity and that this has all happened to me, and to us.

I FEEL LIKE WHAT
IN THE FUTURE A
GO, WE'LL ALWAYS
tHAT WE WENT t
toGE

ER HAPPENS

HOWEVER THINGS

AVE IT IN COMMON

UGH THIS

THER.

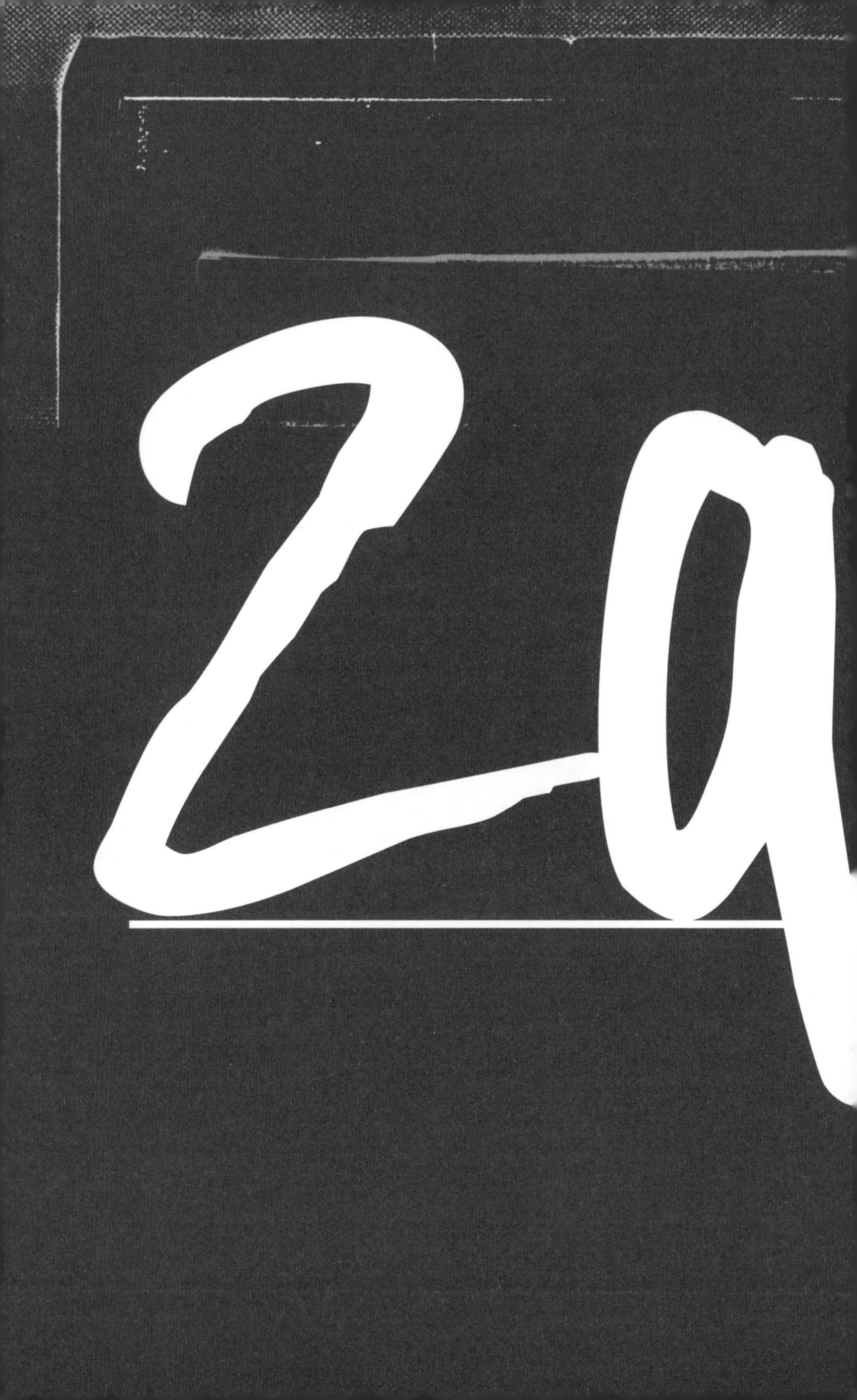

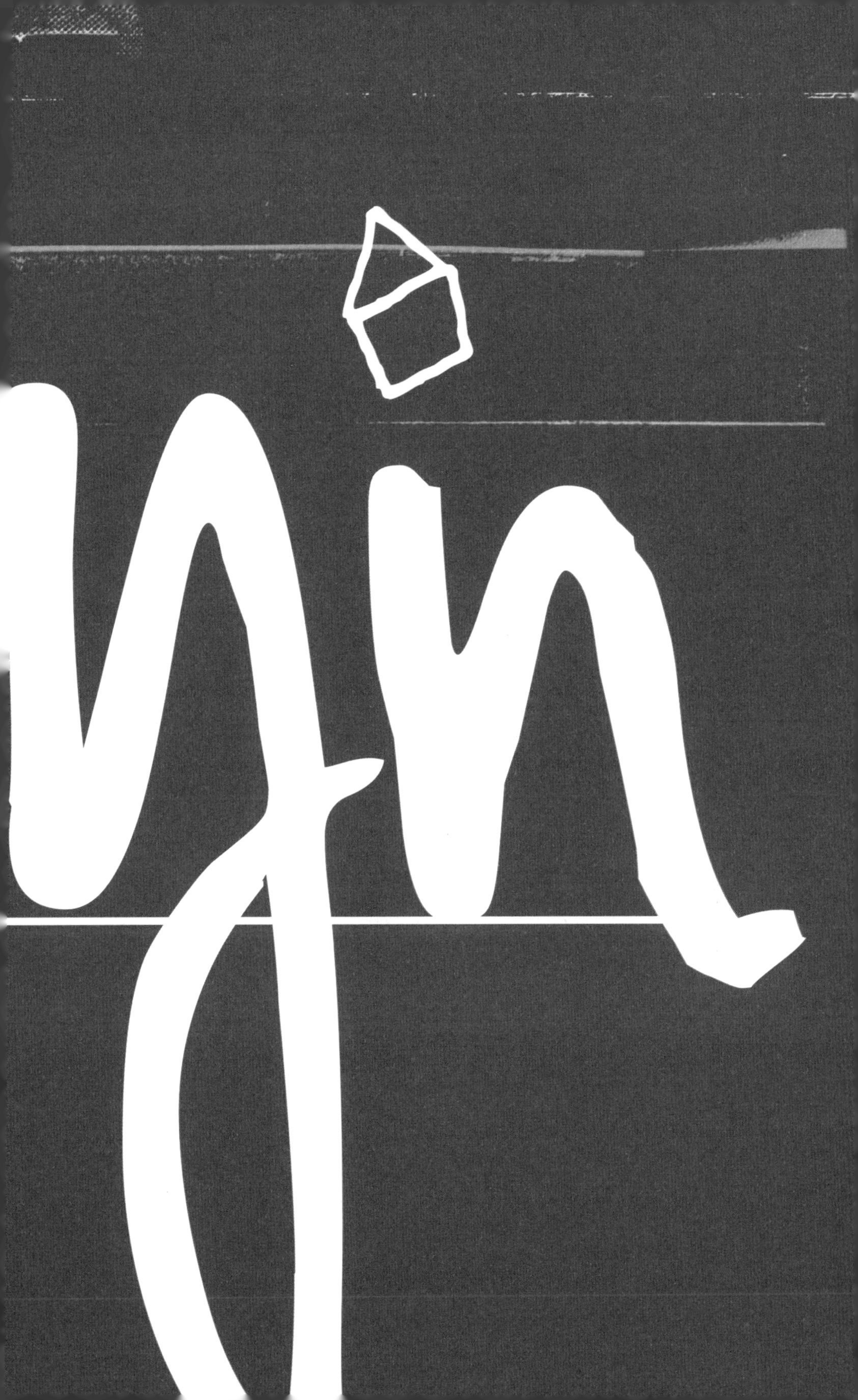

'm lucky enough to come from a large and very close family, so I've got mostly fantastic memories of my childhood. Growing up in Bradford, a town in the north of England, was interesting and sometimes a bit of a challenge. It's a great area, and the sense of community and family is very strong there. When I was a kid, though, there were quite a few new families arriving and some moving on too, so the community was changing fairly rapidly.

This had an impact on me simply because I'm mixed race. As a really young kid, it never crossed my mind that being Irish/English/Asian might cause some people an issue – I was just having a great time playing with my three sisters and friends. But as I got older, a few kids started asking questions, and that's when I began to realise that some of them thought I was – how can I put it? – different.

Kids always like to put things in a category – it's just a part of childhood and growing up in a way, because it helps them understand stuff that's around them. It's not a bad thing. It's just the way kids are. Kids are inquisitive. That's fine when you're at school and someone's asking you which football team you support or what bands you're into, but when I started to get a little older and joined in with various social groups at school, some of the kids started asking me questions that I just didn't understand. 'Where are your parents from?' or 'Where are you from?' as well as 'Why is your mum white and your dad brown?' I can honestly say that when they asked that last one it had never even crossed my mind before, so I didn't actually know what to say in reply.

I was confused. Not confused about who I was and what was important to me, but about why these kids were even

interested in this stuff in the first place. I couldn't understand why it had any relevance. It was baffling. I just thought, *Why do you find that so interesting? What does it matter to you? My mum's my mum and my dad's my dad.*

As a kid I tended to stick to myself, if you like. I like my own space, and I like having the freedom to be who I am and do things my own way. Being the only boy in a family with three sisters meant I spent a fair bit of time on my own at home playing in my room – on computer games, reading comics – boy stuff! I enjoyed school but I didn't have dozens of mates, just a couple of really good ones. I always seemed to have that independent streak.

101.0-2094-3031-3, 0-2276-5035-9 Fax.0-2694-

Growing up with my sisters Safaa, Waliyha and Doniya was a very happy time for me.

It's really interesting how that independence developed as I got older. Before my teenage years I knew that certain kids thought I was different and that sometimes caused problems. You obviously want to be accepted in some way as a kid – no one wants to be left out. Once I hit my teens, though, I started to embrace that feeling of being 'different'. I realised that it was actually kinda cool to be different! By the time I was 15, I *enjoyed* it.

When One Direction took off I had grown into a more confident lad. I was happy within myself. The music and entertainment business is such a varied and interesting place to work too, and there are so many people you meet who are individual. In fact, in the music business being 'different' is applauded and encouraged. So I can honestly say that since the band started, it's never been an issue. In terms of the people I surround myself with – band mates, management, everyone in the behind-the-scenes team – I've never experienced that again. Now I'm getting into my 20s, I can see that any adversity I experienced as a kid has made me who I am.

I was a tough little kid, though, and, as I've explained before, I was extremely hyperactive when I was younger. I used to be bouncing off the walls all over the place, the sort of kid that was always laughing and joking, constantly trying to do something to annoy somebody! My mum was so incredibly patient but she'd still be like, 'Zayn! Calm down! Sit still please!' but I was just impossible to keep still for more than five seconds. It reached a point where my mum didn't know what to do to keep me occupied so she took me to the doctor to try to find out what she should do. They did all these tests and eventually decided that it was some kind of intolerance

Birthday fun with my sisters.

like

a

boss

of vitamin C that was causing the hyperactivity. If I ate something full of that vitamin I'd literally go crazy. So I was told not to eat oranges or any other fruit with vitamin C in it, that sort of stuff, which really helped. I mellowed out as I got older. Around the age of 17 or 18 I naturally just calmed down – ironically, mostly while I was on *The X Factor*.

By the time I was on the show I'd been performing for quite a few years. I sang in choirs back in primary school and loved the experience. I was about 12 when I got into the performing arts. I'm not sure if my initial motivation was something a singing teacher would necessarily approve of, though, because it wasn't about being on stage at first! I went to a performing arts school and quite quickly noticed that a lot of lads were interested in acting and performing; it wasn't just a girly subject, which was how most lads my age thought about it. Then I realised that if you were involved in all these classes and productions, you seemed to get a lot of female attention! I thought to myself, *All the older, fit girls will know who I am!* The ratio of girls to boys was also heavily weighted in my favour too, so I was well up for these classes.

Really quickly after I started the classes, though, I forgot about that flirty motivation because I just loved performing so much. I was totally into it straight away and I found it much more enjoyable than conventional schoolwork. I was quite good in normal classes, actually, and I got 11 GCSEs. So from that point of view I did OK. From time to time my parents would ask me what I fancied doing as a career, and I always said what I really enjoyed more than anything was being on stage and performing. They always replied by saying they'd back me all the way.

At that young age I was actually as much into acting as I was into singing. I ended up appearing in a number of productions, such as *Bugsy Malone* and *Grease*, among others. I loved being on stage playing a different character and doing different accents. For the first time it gave me a chance to channel that energy, the hyperactivity, into doing something creative. The quiet and reserved part of me also loved the opportunity to be more outgoing under the veil of someone else's fictional character.

In my teens I started to get into music big-time. I tended to listen to a lot of R&B, so when I began to watch *The X Factor* and think about maybe auditioning, that was always going to be the type of music I wanted to sing. I studied the show a little bit and thought that there had never really been a person on *The X Factor* before who'd been given a chance to do anything with R&B. I thought if I tried that approach it would be something a little bit . . . different. That word again.

I actually think that's why I got through my first auditions, 'cos I was singing songs that maybe other people weren't choosing at my age. I was singing R&B 90s tunes and there didn't seem to be any other lads that were doing that. I wanted to be the first person in the show to try that style and I figured it would be cool for a young lad of 17 to be able to explore that more left-field type of music. It was quite a brave approach for someone of my age, I think. Obviously, a different opportunity arose for me when they said they wanted to put me in the band. That was a pretty simple decision. I thought, *I'm either gonna go home right now or try this.* I knew it was a massive opportunity so I gave it a go . . . it seems to have worked out OK so far!

This makes me sound more calculating than I actually was. I was never that deliberate. At that age – and in fact through pretty much all of my childhood – I was just a bit of a dreamer. I did have big aspirations for myself and I dreamt that hopefully it might happen for me one day in some way, so my attitude was always, *Let's give it a go.* I wouldn't say I was driven or highly ambitious, though. In fact, I know I wasn't 'superdriven' because even on my audition day for *The X Factor* I didn't wanna get out of bed to go to the show! I think the fact I was a dreamer is nice – it shows my innocence at that age and it reflects really well on my family that I was brought up to believe I *could* pursue my dreams. Whenever I did performances, at school or anywhere else, Mum and Dad were always there, watching and supporting. They always said, 'Zayn, follow your dreams.' That's an amazing attitude and it's had a significant impact on my life. I'm very grateful for it.

You all know what happened on *The X Factor* – it was the most amazing time! Obviously, there was also a really low point too – losing my granddad during the show. That was a really hard, weird time. When you're on that show you're living in a bubble – it's difficult to explain. Nobody really gets it unless they've been in that environment too. You've hardly any contact with the outside world for weeks, and you're not doing anything except for working, rehearsing, interviewing, routining – there's really no time for anything else. You might see your family for maybe an hour after the show on the Saturday, and then that's it – straight back into rehearsals the next day. For a time the outside world almost stops spinning.

Then I got this phone call to say my granddad – who I adored – had died. He'd been ill for some time and knew he

Guess who's getting stuck into the 1D Book Signing?

My Mum was so incredibly patient but she'd still be like, 'Zayn! Calm Down Sit Still Please!'

wasn't gonna make it, but it was still a huge shock. It was just a weird thing to go through. As I've said, I've got a good relationship with my family – they're really close and supportive. That really helped, but because I was on the show it was a time of really odd contrasts. In fact, because of all the madness going on with the show, losing my granddad didn't really sink in until a few months later. I was at home talking to my mum about bits and pieces, then I went upstairs into my bedroom and suddenly everything came flooding back. I was like, 'Oh no, I'm not going to see Granddad again . . .' That was a really low moment.

He was such a cool man. He actually requested 'You Are So Beautiful', one of the songs that One Direction sang on *The X Factor*, to be played at his funeral. That was typical of him, mixing the good with the bad. I wanted to make a gesture of remembrance when we lost him, so that's when I got my first tattoo. It's on my right chest and is simply his name.

While we're on the subject of tattoos, you may have noticed I've had quite a few! I love getting tattoos and I really enjoy the whole culture around them too. I like going to the tattoo parlour, meeting all these interesting people, being involved in all that. When I had that first one done for my granddad I realised that it wasn't actually that painful, so I immediately wanted more. I'm currently working on a full sleeve and I've found a really cool guy in LA who does all my work. I like the fact that tattoos allow me to say something without physically saying something – you know what I mean? I'm not one for making big, loud announcements, drawing attention to myself, all that. Tattoos are not so much a statement – I see mine as more like me saying something

ZAYN

to myself, creating a little visual memento to remind me of a certain important time in my life. A quiet reminder.

Anyway, back to One Direction. We signed our record deal pretty quickly after the show and that was just mad. My main worry was that we'd only come third. I felt we'd done really well, but I was saying to the lads, 'We're all very aware that there are no guarantees about succeeding, or even getting a record deal here, boys.' So to sign the contract was a great starting point. I knew we had so much work to do before we could even put out a single, but at least we had a chance.

The five of us had a tight chemistry almost from the word go. To backtrack a little bit, I felt we really clicked the first time when we met up at Harry's step-dad's bungalow. I arrived late 'cos I had some family stuff going on. While that was sorted, my dad was saying to me that maybe I didn't need to go to the rehearsals yet. He was going, 'You can spend a bit more time at home before you go off.' I wonder if he knew then that if the band worked I'd be leaving home pretty much for good? Maybe he was trying to hold on to me ...

Anyway, I needed to go, we had to rehearse and there was work to do. Louis came to my house to pick me up. He came straight up to where I lived and parked right outside my house in his little Renault Clio. He shouted, 'Come on, Zayn!' so I ran out and jumped in the car. He was driving pretty crazy, doing all this mad stuff and I was thinking straight away, *He's a funny lad!* On the way to Harry's we ended up nearly having a crash on the motorway but, to be fair to him, there was some good driving, and we swerved it out and survived! Joking aside, I knew straight away that I was gonna get on with him, 'cos Louis is just one of the lads.

the boys, with
the other boys
@5SOS

We got to the bungalow and it was a bit odd at first 'cos the lads were like, 'Why haven't you been here the last coupla days?' but then after that we got on great. I spent virtually the whole time at that bungalow laughing. For me, after that, I realised it wasn't gonna be that hard to get on with these lads. We just seemed to click straight away.

The first few weeks of PAs and club shows after *The X Factor* was a really intense time. We were fresh out of the show, so everything felt new to us. We were doing these little gigs up and down the country, playing in all these weird places with about 250 people crammed in – mad times. What completely amazed me was how girls were going faint when we turned up. I was saying to the lads, 'I don't understand why they're doing that or, to be completely honest, how they even know who we are.' I kept having to remind myself that we'd just spent weeks and weeks on the biggest show on British telly. People had been watching us perform every week. I'd watched *The X Factor* for many years too and I understand that as the weeks go by the viewers feel like they're really getting to know the contestants. At the time, one of our managers said to me, 'Zayn, the girls at those shows feel a real intimacy with the band. You're only just starting to meet your fans, but they feel like they've known you for months.' I get that now but at first it was a bit of a shock. I was baffled and thought what was happening was crazy.

I'm really lucky that being in One Direction has allowed me to travel all over the world. I've been to countries and seen cultures and ways of life that are just amazing to be around, to learn from and to soak up. When the band first started, though, I didn't even have a passport, let alone flown on a plane! I'll be totally honest – I'd never even seen a train. That makes it sound like Bradford is some tiny little village hundreds of miles from anywhere! It isn't; it's a big place, but the simple fact is that at Bradford Interchange, where I used to get my bus every day, if I'd just walked round the back there's a train station! I'd just never bothered to go and have a look. I got my bus to classes and then went out locally. I'd never actually ever left Bradford.

So when we all piled on to the plane to head out to LA for our first ever recording session as One Direction, yes, I was the most nervous. Those nerves weren't helped by the lads telling me, 'The plane's gonna do loop the loops and all these mad stunts in the air.' I was crapping myself! Thanks, lads!

Recording in LA and Sweden was a real eye-opener for me. Some of the lads had been to the States on holiday before, but it was all new to me and I was proper excited. Even meeting American people for the first time was an interesting experience – trying to understand their accents, their slang, it was fascinating.

Also, I'd never been in a studio before (apart from the *X Factor* winner's single, which was just so quick anyway). I didn't even know how to sing in a booth using a studio mike, 'cos that's completely different to singing on stage without headphones. You really have to concentrate on every syllable that comes out of your mouth, because those mikes are so incredibly sensitive and they pick up on everything, every little detail. Effectively, you have to learn a new way to sing, and it's far more technical and on the button than singing live.

The producers for those early sessions were meticulous. Everything had to be sung in a certain way, it had to sound

ZAYN

exactly right, and their attention to detail and perfectionism was incredible. They would sometimes focus on just one word for what seemed like hours, making sure it sounded perfect.

That proved to be quite a challenge for me, though. The type of singer I am means I often hear different melodies in my head. I'll hear a song's melody and immediately alternative tunes will suggest themselves. On stage that's great, because I've the opportunity to improvise and change things around, but in the studio you need to be very precise. So at times I admit I found that really hard. I'd sometimes have my own version of a melody stuck in my head and we'd have to record my lines fifty times to keep it faithful to the original idea. That was really difficult to start off with. The producers were so focused – they just wanted everything to be perfect and, let's face it, 'What Makes You Beautiful' was the result!

For our first single that song was perfect. I felt it was a really great pop song. In fact, we all felt the same way about it. It wasn't so much that I thought it was going to go to Number 1 all around the world; I just thought it was a true representation of us five lads at that point in time. We didn't care about girls wearing make-up – still don't. Some pop songs can have quite questionable underlying themes, but we didn't want to get involved with any of that. If I'm being totally honest with you, all these years later that song should feel a little awkward to sing, because I've moved on and grown up, but even so, it's such a big song for us as a band that when we do perform it live the crowd goes mental and we really get into it. We were very lucky to have 'What Makes You Beautiful' as our début single and even luckier to see it go to Number 1 in the UK. What an amazing start!

Very quickly, life in One Direction became completely mad. Being mobbed at Heathrow Airport was a big one – that was insane. We had our jumpers ripped off us, literally pulled off our backs – that whole experience was the craziest thing ever. I said to the lads at the time, 'I never thought I'd see that happen to somebody else, never mind myself.' When we'd been doing PAs and then the *X Factor* tour, sometimes girls would chase our car down the road afterwards, it was just mad from the word go. There were always so many fans out there waiting to meet us, they were just incredible. Heathrow took it to a whole new level, though. At that point, before the single had even come out, I was starting to think that maybe something big was happening.

Funnily enough, people tend to assume One Direction has been nothing but plain sailing, and to a certain extent that's true. But I do remember feeling pretty vulnerable when our second single, 'Gotta Be You', was less well received than 'What Makes You Beautiful'. We'd got it so right on that first single, but for the follow-up I didn't feel we were so spot on. I remember saying to the lads one day, 'The video doesn't feel right to me. I'm not convinced this whole single is going to work the same way.' People were quite into the song, but it wasn't perceived in the right way by everyone. Although the single hit Number 3, which was brilliant, there was a worry. I was like, 'Lads, do you think that maybe we've already peaked? Maybe this is all going to fizzle out as fast as it took off? Maybe we've had our time? Maybe this isn't going to be as big as some people have been suggesting?' To have failed at that stage, having already tasted some of the highs, would've been devastating.

238

Fortunately, we had a secret weapon – our amazing fans! One Direction fans are unique – they really are an army championing us all around the world. Back in the really early days, the power of our fans on social media was staggering. We would all constantly recognise that – 'Can you quite believe what these fans are doing for us?!' There's a saying, 'right place, right time', and I definitely think we benefited from that in terms of our fans and the opportunity for them to talk about us online. That was a huge factor in our early success.

I've a theory about social media and our generation. I don't want to get too deep here, but at the same time I think it's an important reason why One Direction have enjoyed so much success. Plus I want to acknowledge the role our fans have played in our story. Ours is a whole new generation of kids who feel like this is our era. The people in each decade have their own style, and when we started off as a band the kids in our generation had social media – that was *ours*. There was that sense of 'We're gonna take control of all this. Now this is our time.' That's how this generation deals with stuff in our lives – everything we do is based around our social networks. Every opinion we have now is gonna be put on social networks and this is how we tell other people about every band we like. We all connect with the whole world through Twitter, Facebook and more recently Instagram. These are all sites on which our generation chats to each other. Instead of just chatting to mates locally, we can talk to people on the other side of the world as well. So what this generation has done is make the whole world our community.

All these things came together just before and then during the time we formed as a band. What that meant for One

Direction was that when our fans started to talk about us online early on, the whole world heard them talking. It was crazy enough being on the biggest TV show in the UK, but 'cos the UK is pretty influential on Twitter, people out there look in to see what Brits are saying, and suddenly we were being spoken about globally. Once our fans started discussing us on social media, the scale of the thing blew up massive. That's a major reason why we took off so quickly, perhaps in a way that no other band had ever done before (not necessarily in terms of scale but in terms of how it happened). Maybe we were the first band to benefit from the full power of that new platform? I don't know, I could be reading too much into it. What I do know is that once our fans got onto social media, things were never the same again.

For me, the début album *Up All Night* is a real record of its time. We might not sing quite so high these days and maybe the lyrics we write now have changed in tone because we're older, but that record is a really authentic reflection of where we were as a band and as five lads at that exact point in our lives. It still has some really good pop songs on there. The fact that it was a Number 1 record and did so well for us around the world is a big achievement. We were only kids. It was a big deal to get that record out and for it to do so well. I'm really proud of that album.

The headline tour to promote the début album was fantastic. We'd done those PA shows, the *X Factor* tour, a lot of promo performances, but nothing compared with that theatre tour. At that point I wasn't getting much sleep – none of us were. It was pretty hardcore! We'd finish work really late at

night, sometimes into the next morning, and then catch a few hours' sleep before getting up for the early radio shows or morning TV, crack of dawn, then promo all day till the next gig. I was just running on adrenalin constantly. It was brilliant!

It's a mad thing to go through, and at times the only thing that keeps you sane is the fact you have four other lads doing the same thing, experiencing the same feelings and events with you. I'm really lucky in that sense. Although I'm a quiet and independent person by nature, I'm really glad that I'm not by myself for this whole experience. I don't have to sit alone on the tour bus after a show, thinking these things through. I feel that sense of camaraderie most when we're on the road – even as far back as that first tour, we were just such a tight unit. It's times like those on the road when I really see One Direction as my gang.

I think the public see that too. Maybe that's part of our appeal. Hopefully, they know we have a genuine relationship behind the scenes. Bands can easily portray themselves as mates on TV or in a music video, but we actually have that as five friends – and it's a good feeling. I believe people can see when it's fake. They see straight through the pretence. We take the mick out of each other like normal mates would. Also, we aren't trying to be the best of friends living in some pop band utopia. If we disagree about something we'll have a squabble about it for half an hour, and then we'll come back and say sorry.

We still have the same laughs now. If I wasn't in this group I'd look and think, *I wish I was mates with them lads*. We're definitely a bit of a gang, and we have our in-jokes and band humour. It's a bit of a private club at times, but that often helps us get through the crazy stuff. I do realise it can be a little daunting when people meet all five of us together – we can take the mick and all that, but it's a good place to be when you're in that gang.

Next up for us was our first trip to the States. That was a big shock 'cos we didn't really know what to expect. The US is such a big place: the geography, the population, the massive number of radio stations, venues, the scale of the promotion you've got to do. It's just this huge challenge. But you know what? We were like, 'We can't get stuck in fast enough!'

We had the *Big Time Rush* support tour booked, so we were driving around in this battered van and staying in some pretty dingy hotels. It was like, 'I don't fancy your room much, Liam!' There were quite a few weird places on those dates! From the very first gig those fans knew every single word of every song. When we finished each night's set we'd get outside and jump on this rusty little tour bus and all these girls would be running out of the arena, chasing our bus down the road. We'd be looking out of the bus windows, just shaking our heads in disbelief, really. 'What is going on here?' It was just so odd to see. Brilliant, of course – but odd. We almost had to say it out loud to each other to try and comprehend what we were witnessing: 'OK, these people live in North America. How come they know every single word?' It was really that confusing.

We did a signing at a shopping mall during all this early promo and a girl gave me a CD to sign. I took the CD off her and as I did my hand must've touched hers ... and instantly she stone cold fainted, flat out, right on the spot. She literally dropped to the floor, lights out. I'd never seen anything like that in my life – I couldn't believe it. I saw her eyes go and went to grab her hand, but she was already on the floor. I didn't even know what was happening. The security came and had to physically lift her off the floor as she was out cold. I hadn't got a clue what was happening. The lads said you could see it in my face. I was completely bewildered, thinking, *Did that really just happen?* I said to the lads, 'I've never seen anything like that happen before, for a start, but also I'd only expect that to happen with someone like Michael Jackson or Elvis when they were alive. Never ever in a million years would I expect someone to react in such an extreme way to meeting me.' It was just the weirdest thing. I couldn't really process that back then, and to be totally honest, I still can't now.

The States was so exciting. Every minute of every day was a new adventure – it was relentless and just brilliant. My life was moving so fast and everything was so insane, but I tried to remember how important it was to keep in touch with family and friends, to never forget that. You have to make time for these people – they're so important.

Of course, the One Direction juggernaut was not about to stop. 'What Makes You Beautiful' got into the US Top 30 and we also won a Brit Award, which was crazy. Then they decided to release our début album a week early in the US 'cos it was all kicking off for us.

Initially I had very little expectation for the album. Then we started to hear people talking about big pre-sales and indications that fans were gonna buy a lot of copies. Personally, once I realised there was a chance, however small, of that

B stage in Melbourne!!!

album being Number 1, I was like, 'Let's just do everything in our power to get it there.' We wanted to be the first UK band to do that with a début album. We were mad hungry.

So we did every interview, went to every radio station, made every appearance and got on every TV show we could. Any promo that might possibly help sales was instantly agreed to, that gang mentality came in again, and as a collective of five lads with this team behind us it was pretty powerful.

The *Today* show appearance during the week of the album's release was a strangely amazing experience to try to compute. The actual performance itself was great fun and we did a good job, I think. The setting in New York was ridiculous, but it was just the sheer scale of the crowd that was incredible. I was singing and looking around, and found myself thinking of all those individual stories behind everyone who was there. All those train journeys, bus journeys, time off school, college or work, money spent on travel and food, even back to getting ready at home to come out to see us. I just kept saying, 'It's just so much effort by so many people.' That's crazy if just one person does that for your band, but when you're confronted by thousands of people doing that it's just the most humbling feeling. This wasn't even a full gig, remember, it was just a TV appearance. The effort people had to make to be standing in that street right there and then ... *wow!* If I think about the amount of effort by that number of people, to be honest, it can blow my mind.

When I got the phone call that we'd got the Number 1, I was in my hotel room having a lie-in. The other lads had gone out somewhere and I'd just been catching up on some kip when the phone rang and someone from management said,

WE'D BE LOOKING
WINDOWS, JUST SH
DISBELIEF, REALLY.
"WHAT IS
ON HER

t OF THE BUS
ING OUR HEADS IN

GOING
E?

#1dtodayshow we're live!!!!!

'Zayn, great news. It's Number 1!' I didn't want to go back to sleep after that call! It's mad that we'd done something no other British band had done before. We knew it was a big deal, but there wasn't really time for that sense of achievement to sink in – like with most of the stuff that's happened in One Direction's career, to be honest. As we carried on with promo, all the TV presenters, radio people and journalists kept saying, 'One Direction is the first British band to début at Number 1 in the US,' so over the course of a few weeks it gradually did start to register. It still feels amazing, though. You look back at all the incredible bands that haven't done what we did, and it's just a bizarre thing, really. I can't really put it into words how that made me feel.

The rest of 2012 was just the most insane blizzard of events. We met Michelle Obama, we toured in support of the album all over, did loads of promo and TV – it was relentless. We were loving it, though. Tiring? Yes. Not enjoyable? Never.

A stand-out One Direction moment from that summer was obviously the Olympics. The performance was intense, as we were all standing on the back of a truck in that huge stadium with the eyes of the world watching. A couple of nights before the Olympics, my girlfriend was dyeing her hair peroxide blonde and I just said, 'It will be funny to shove a bit of blond in my hair at the front!' So I just did it for a bit of a laugh and made this big massive blond streak. Then I realised I'd the Olympics in a coupla days and I was like, 'What am I gonna do?!' I tried to style it out but it wasn't happening, so in the end I just left it. Part of me was singing on that truck and thinking, *I hope people don't cuss me for this blond streak!*

Turned out people liked it. Then, bizarrely, Marvel Comics said that my look had inspired the new version of Ghost Rider. The blond streak is the fire that ignites from him, which is mad. I'm a big comic book fan – when I was a kid I was pretty geeky about all that. Obviously, I also have my 'Zap!' tattoo on my forearm, so when I heard about the new Ghost Rider that was pretty cool. I've since been to the Marvel Studios, which was an amazing experience.

Backstage at the Olympics was mad. These crazily famous people were coming and talking to me. I've grown up my whole life seeing them on TV and here they were just chatting away to us – the Spice Girls, Madness, Russell Brand, Liam Gallagher, properly famous people. Russell Brand was brilliant. He was saying, 'Your performance was sick,' and then he started giving me family planning advice! I was like, 'Russell, you shouldn't be giving me that sort of advice!' He was hilarious, a really nice guy.

The Olympics was the start of a lot of craziness. It was when I started to realise that famous people – celebrities, high-profile individuals – recognised us. There were even a few who seemed shy around us, a bit nervous to meet us. How daft is that? Nuts!

Throughout all of this, we were writing for the second album. We did sessions in LA, Sweden and some work in London too. This time around we wanted to make the new album a bit more personal, put more of ourselves into it. We wanted to really make it our own. Part of that was 'cos we now knew that we'd have to sing these songs for years to come. I was very much of this opinion, and went, 'These songs have to mean something to us. This is important.'

I was really happy with that album once we'd finished. Songs like 'Live While We're Young' were, for me anyway, a real progression. It felt like there was a cooler edge to the record. There was still that energy, that buzz, but it had somehow evolved and, like the first album, the music really reflected where we were as a band and as five individuals at that point. We really enjoyed promoting that record, which I think is down to making sure the songs were totally personal.

This also made it all the more special when that second album hit Number 1 in so many countries. It was a vindication of our efforts – all that time spent writing songs on the road, the extra hours, and trying to find the right lyric or melody. It had all been worth it and we were really proud. To get another Number 1 in the States was also a big achievement – with the expectation for this record being on a whole other level to the first album, there had been pressure to succeed, but we kept our heads down, worked away and it panned out for us.

We've all spoken about Madison Square Garden before but it really was a special moment for the band. Not just us five, but everyone involved in One Direction. From my perspective it was quite an odd gig in terms of seeing these really famous people wanting to come and meet us. Chris Rock was there with his kids – that was exciting and he was really cool. You begin to realise these are just normal people with families of their own, and that the fame thing is just part of their job. Then the legendary film director Martin Scorsese walks into our dressing room. There's not much you can say about that, is there?

This all injects an extra bit of adrenalin into the show. You might think that walking out on stage is all we have to do –

and it's certainly the most important part of the night – but before that we've been backstage meeting all these famous people, trying to acclimatise to chatting with these super-stars, then doing maybe some promo, a soundcheck, meet-and-greets, getting ready, all that. You've gotta take all of this in and then make sure that when you get up on stage it's perfect. That whole experience really adds to the whole vibe of a big gig like MSG or the Olympics. I love it.

Sometimes I'm not entirely comfortable with the high-profile nature of my job. I'm quite a private person, and I think that's why when I was a kid I used to really enjoy acting. I loved the fact that when I was in a play or a musical I was playing a character, portraying someone else. In One Direc-tion, though, I'm not playing a character. I'm just being myself, so that's a completely different experience. That's why I come across as more shy at times. I'm not being somebody else – I'm just myself. To a degree that means I'm more exposed. I understand that dynamic, but it's OK. I really try to take care over what I say and do, as I really don't want to offend anyone or cause problems, but that's not always possible. People forget we're just regular lads, growing up, and occasionally messing up. It can feel like a lot of pressure but what we've always tried to do is do our best by our fans. I just want to get on with our music. Writing, recording and performing – that's what I enjoy most in all this.

I certainly don't see myself as a celebrity. Why would I? I understand we're in a high-profile band, but so what? In a way, I'm not even sure there is such a specific thing as a celebrity. You shouldn't really have a tag just because you're on telly or sing songs or act in films. I don't think it's even a

#zaynmalik and his mum

cool tag to have, not like being a doctor or nurse or fireman, jobs like that. So it always bemuses me when people say they want to be a celebrity.

I wouldn't ever want to be called a celebrity. The more I meet really famous people, the more I don't see them in that way. They're normal people. Famous people who I'm a fan of are important in my life, though. That's because they're influential to me, they're people who I've taken or learned something from, or who've made me rethink something. If One Direction have any impact on people's lives, then maybe that's the best thing we can do – I'm not talking about being influential in politics or anything on that level. Maybe we can just have a positive impact on a few people's lives. Maybe we'll make them look at music in a different light. Maybe we'll even make them want to write songs, sing live, perform. Or maybe we might just affect their lives in some small way that they appreciate and enjoy. That would be amazing.

After Christmas 2012 the work was only just beginning for the year ahead, because in 2013 we'd this massive tour planned to support the new album – in fact, around 130 shows in total. That tour was mad, simply because I don't think I was really ready to go away for that length of time. In my own head I was still processing everything that had happened to us and it would've perhaps been nice to have had a break and take in the first album campaign before we started on the second. Obviously, that's not the way things work with One Direction, so we just kept going!

I remember halfway through that tour it got a little difficult for me. One of the lads asked me what was up and I replied,

'I'm just feeling really homesick and missing home.' I was still really enjoying each gig and meeting the fans – that was never negative in any way – the lads would ask if I was OK and like I said, I'd reply, 'I just miss my family.' I craved being in my own home in my own surroundings. It's funny how long jaunts on the road affect you – simple things like missing the comfort of sitting on your own sofa can become frustrating. It messes with your head sometimes.

But, just to be clear, I'd never complain about touring. We are 100 per cent grateful for everything we've been given. It's just that occasionally it's difficult to balance it with your life when you're so young and don't have much life experience.

That tour was a long time out on the road and, being completely open with you, it did occasionally take its toll on one or other of us at some point. At times I felt homesick, and I missed family and friends. As you guys know, by now I was also in a relationship with Perrie Edwards, someone very special to me – and so that was hard. When you've met someone who means so much to you, being away from them for long periods of time is really difficult. In August 2013 we got engaged – I know people are really interested in the details and our plans together, but I always prefer to keep that private. It's just my nature to be like that. Back then, on tour for such a long spell, I missed Perrie really badly so there were times when, on a personal level, I was feeling pretty deflated.

Again, though, this was when the One Direction gang mentality came into its own. We'd just close ranks and pick up whoever was feeling homesick or tired or down, and off we'd go again. I've heard it said that the best bands are gangs, and I really believe that. We're a gang and, whatever happens in the future, we'll always be a gang. Even if in 50 years' time, if one of us is doing a project without the others, I'd like to be there to support them.

By stark contrast to all the One Direction madness, we had a massive reality check when we went to Ghana for Comic Relief. That was just the most emotional, heartbreaking experience of my life. I'd never seen poverty like that and it was really hard to keep it together. I just came away from that thinking how lucky we all are to have the lives we do. Not just the lads in One Direction, I mean everyone who isn't in that situation. That was the ultimate perspective among all this mad band stuff we were experiencing. It was a privilege to meet those people.

Throughout the year we'd also been filming the movie, *This Is Us*, with cameras following us pretty much the whole time on the road from the shows at the O2 onwards. For me, the movie idea was appealing in the sense that I'm a bit of a photo and video freak, a visual hoarder if you like. It was just drilled into me from when I was a kid to get photos, shoot video – my parents always said that this stuff is important. They were like crazy tourists with massive cameras hanging around their necks wherever we went, even just birthday parties at home. They always had a camera flashing or a video filming. They were constantly taking pictures of every move I made! I picked up on this and always get anxious if I think I've not captured something important. I like to keep memories of life.

So when the idea of a film of the band was presented to me, I was really excited because I thought in 15 years' time we'd be able to look back on all this madness and have a brilliant record of what we'd done. It's easy to remember the

Food on the run

big moments, the massive gigs, the TV shows, award ceremonies and all that, but there's so much other stuff that goes on that's equally important in its own way. Mad things like messing about on the tour bus, dumb stuff backstage, the laughs we have. I'm usually trying to film it all, but for once it was great to have someone else thinking about the camera!

We had no dialogue, no scripts – the entire film was just captured as it happened. I didn't care if they followed me to the toilet, although that might not have made the final cut, perhaps! Seriously, though, it was genuinely access all areas, as we were keen to make sure that the movie was as real as possible. In a way you might think that this would be tiring, but because we're never trying to be anything other than what we naturally are, it was easy. We just did our stuff, and they happened to be there filming it.

What a buzz at the première too. That was ridiculous. I just look back on that movie and feel very proud to have made it and to have been in the position where a good number of people wanted to see it. I also look forward to that night in 15 or 20 years when I'll sit down and watch it all back.

In typical One Direction style, so much has already happened since the film came out. For starters our third album, *Midnight Memories*, was really well received pretty much all over the world. There just seemed to be a constant increase in the momentum. Just as with the second album, where we'd been determined to get involved in the creative writing process, we also got stuck into writing on the third album. Even more so, in fact. That was harder in a sense because we were on the road so much throughout the year, but we somehow found the time by using mobile studios, improvised set-ups in hotel rooms, just writing all over the place. If you want something badly enough, you'll find the time and the means.

We really wanted that third record to be a further progression and to represent where we were at that point in time. We're never trying to force anything on anybody – we just wanna do what we're doing in our own lives and talk about it through our music. 'Story of My Life' sums it all up really. I'd like to think people would agree our music is getting more mature with us – it's a natural evolution. That's the type of lads we are. We want our music to be right, and we wanna leave the right message and the right statement and be able to look back on it in ten years and go, 'Yes, that's exactly what we were feeling at that time.' With *Midnight Memories* I think we got that right. I hope so, anyway.

We were feeling quite a bit of pressure this time, though. One Direction had enjoyed so much success in so many countries that there was absolutely no way of keeping expectations low this time around. Fortunately the album was a big hit, reaching Number 1 in tons of places across the world. We were so proud of the fans' reaction to those songs. When you put yourself out there in that way, you're a bit exposed. You'll feel any criticism, so that was a big boost for us. Massive.

Ahead of the 2014 stadium tour, we're all so excited. When we first saw the stage at rehearsals it was just stunning. That was a good day, a mad feeling. I didn't know what to expect. I knew the stage was gonna be big, but not THAT big. It's massive! There's a film called *Rock Star* featuring Mark Wahlberg and our set reminds me of one of the stages in that film! I was like, 'Lads, this stage looks sick!'

1D | **ONE**
DIRECTION
THIS IS US

SONY PICTURES RELEASING
HAS PLEASURE IN INVITING

**TO THE PARTY
FOLLOWING THE
WORLD PREMIERE**

TUESDAY AUGUST 20TH

SANDERSON
50 BERNERS STREET
LONDON W1T 3NG

CARRIAGES 1:00AM

NO ADMITTANCE WITHOUT THIS TICKET.
THIS TICKET IS NOT TRANSFERABLE.

We had a little bit of a wobble when the tour was initially announced. We'd put out some promo saying there was going to be a big announcement, and then when we revealed our plans for the stadium tour there were a few people sniping at us, saying it was 'One Big Disappointment', a few negative comments online. Obviously, we'd been a little anxious that we could sell out such massive venues, so that was a bit of a worry. Then my phone rang and it was management. I assumed they were going to say, 'Sorry, Zayn. You've overreached yourselves, I'm afraid. Looks like we aren't gonna sell these places out. We might need to downsize. It was too much of a jump after all. You've got to go back down to arenas for a few more years.' But in fact they actually told me that instead of playing one Wembley Stadium gig we'd need to play three 'cos it was all sold out! That's One Direction fans for you – the best in the world.

We've done two stadiums before, in Mexico, and so with that in mind I'm very excited – and a little bit nervous! – to find out what these colossal stadiums are going to be like to play. I remember one big amphitheatre gig in Verona really well. I was really excited about it, knowing it was the biggest gig we'd done to date. The whole day of the gig I was like, 'Yeah, it's cool. I'm chilled, all under control.' Then the crowd started to filter in, and I could see the numbers getting bigger and bigger. The nerves started to kick in then a little bit. I was thinking, *OK, that's getting a bit big. I'm still cool though. Cool, all good.*

When it came to show time I was still thinking it was all cool, then I ran out on to the stage and BOOM! This massive wall of energy hit me like a truck. Literally, this wave of noise, energy and excitement just smashed into me and completely took my breath away. The stage suddenly seemed enormous and the crowd was so vast I couldn't compute what I was looking at. It was just insane. If I'm totally honest, I felt a little bit out of my depth. I know we'd played some big arenas and all that before, but this was something else. It was such a shock!

We were singing along to the first song and I was still a bit dazed. Then I looked around at the other lads and I was like, 'Yo, lads! This is mad!' We had a bit of a laugh about it and my nerves instantly started to recede. After that it was just the wildest gig.

I'm really excited to be performing in stadiums that are substantially bigger than any venues we've played before. On certain slower songs you get a little bit of time to think and look out at the crowd to soak up what's going on. I know there will be times when I'm looking out on this tour and thinking, *This is insane!* Looking at the size of all the venues, I think that will be the best feeling pretty much every night! I can't wait.

I'm often asked when this whole crazy One Direction experience started to sink in. My honest answer? I don't think it ever sinks in. I'd see myself as a weird person if it did. To me, it would be strange if I ever found this 'normal', because it's not normal. Nothing we're doing is normal.

When people get bored of One Direction and start throwing tomatoes instead of underwear at us, then that'll be the time to put down our guitars and go home! For now, though, we're here to stay.

While working on this book, looking back on what's happened has been quite a process. Like I said before, I don't wanna give myself the tag of being driven or ambitious. I didn't see this opportunity and think, *That's mine for the taking.* It was much more spontaneous than that. I'm here right now and if I'm being completely frank with you, I don't know how I got here. I'm just thankful that I did get here and it's sick that I am. I'm grateful for everything that I've been blessed with in this band. I'm just enjoying it, and I'm as bamboozled as everyone else as to why One Direction are the scale that we are.

I'm not suggesting in any way that we haven't worked for our success. We have, very hard. Nothing in life lands in your lap. From getting up early that day for the *X Factor* audition to our first 2014 stadium show when we walked out having spent months in planning and then rehearsals, it's an intense – at times extreme – amount of work. I do have to work very hard to be in the position that I'm in. So have the rest of the band and everyone around One Direction – we've all put in so many hours and so much effort. At the same time, so many other people have gone out and worked and got in these positions and gone to interviews and auditions and worked hard every day, but they haven't had the same level of success. So in terms of processing exactly how successful we are, that's the difficult part for me. I don't really understand that bit if I'm honest, but I do understand that this band has certainly put in the hard work to have earned it.

As I said earlier, as a kid I was a dreamer. I've always believed that I wanted to do something a little bit extra with myself. I don't know why I thought that. Maybe it was my parents always fuelling those dreams, maybe it was something inside me. I don't know. I just know I had dreams. Luckily, thanks to One Direction and our fans, I'm now living the dream.

269

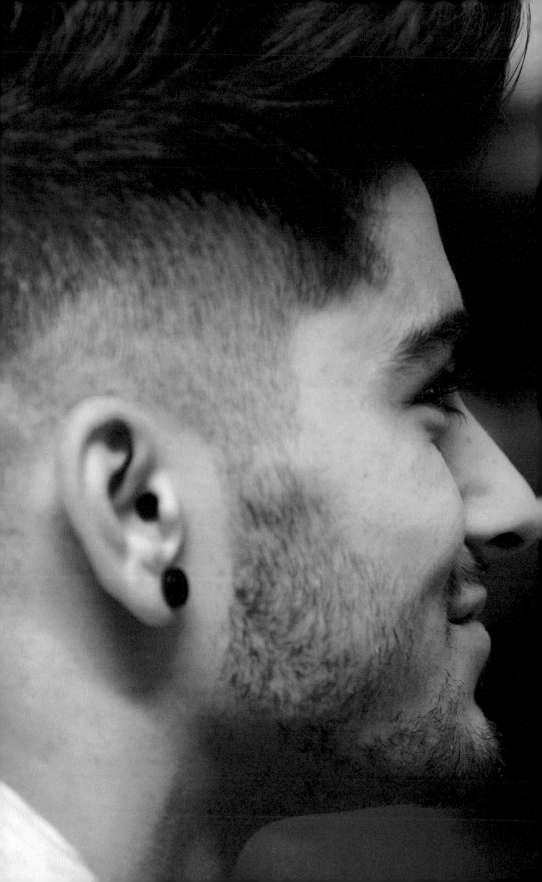

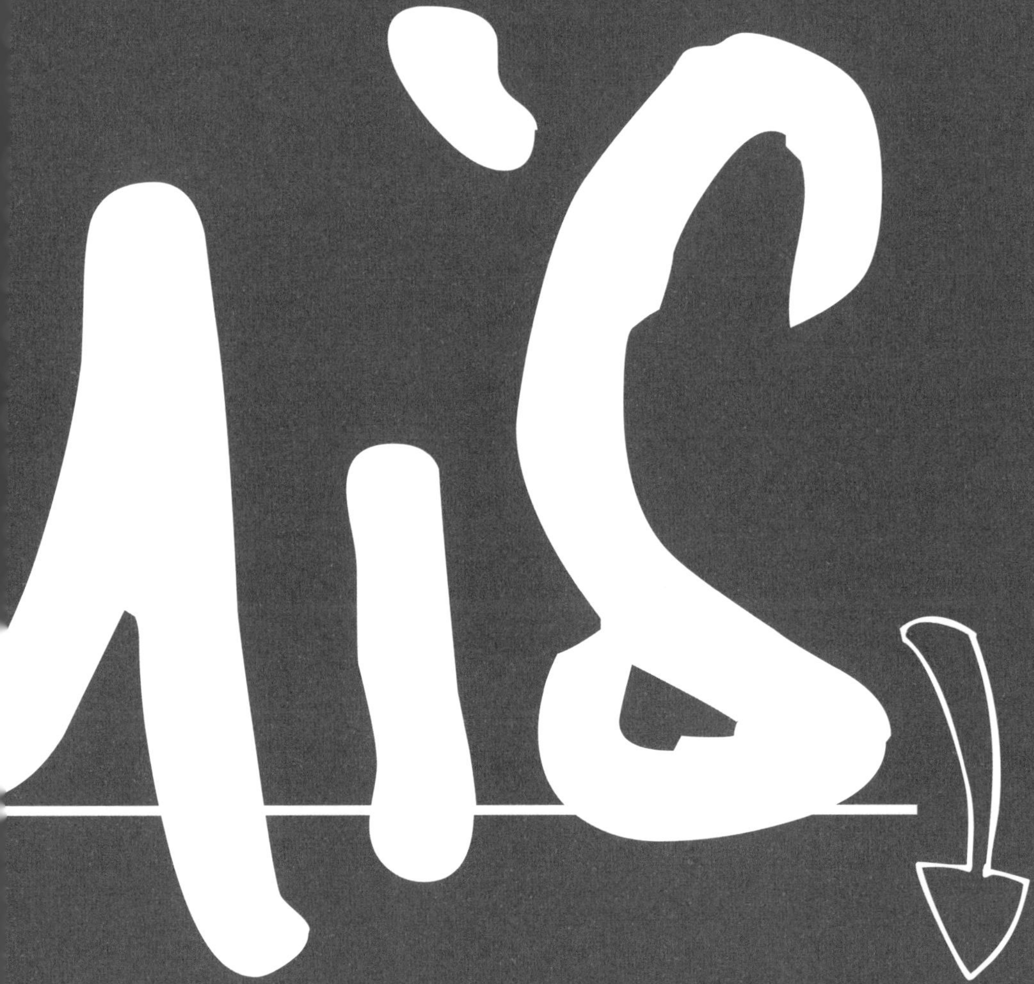

Louis

It's no secret that I was a lively kid who loved performing. I always wanted to be the centre of attention, the class clown, if you like. I come from a big family and I loved to be in the thick of everything that was going on. At school I wasn't great 'cos I didn't put my mind to it. It was the same with my part-time jobs. I got sacked from them for being largely disinterested. It was also the same with college. I hadn't taken school that seriously because I was just in it for the doss, but somehow I got through my GCSEs fine. Naturally, I thought, I'll do the same at A Level, but as so many people find out to their cost, you can't do that!

My heart wasn't really in it and I just wanted to go in to college to see my mates. I loved those times, but I just wasn't the teachers' favourite. Some of the best years of my life were at school and college, and I miss that big time. I just didn't really apply myself academically. However, I clearly remember having a fire in my belly for singing and performing. I never gave anything other than 100 per cent in that respect. Looking back now, I can see that I just needed to find something that I was passionate about.

Obviously, being in One Direction means I travel the world in a way that I could never have thought possible when I was a kid, even though I was always keen to expand my horizons beyond my hometown of Doncaster. All through my teenage years, teachers used to ask me what plans I had for a career and I'd say, 'I kind of assume I'll head off to university and after that probably become a teacher, or maybe do something with sport somewhere.' I loved where I lived, but I was very aware that there weren't necessarily too many opportunities in Doncaster – so I might have to move on somewhere

From as early as I can remember, I enjoyed being the centre of attention!

Top: Making plans in the sand for how to build my first house. On holiday in Bournemouth.
Middle: Defo cut my fringe myself!
Bottom: The original hangover baby.

Louis

9 Fax 0-2694

Top: With my sister Lottie.
Bottom: Loving tea at a young age!

Louis

Top: Buzzing in the bath!
Middle: Me and my lovely nan.
Bottom: Me and a random dog!

else. Never in a million years would I have expected to be travelling as much as I do now, though!

I've been called ambitious and driven, but I never sat down and planned any of this. I'm not the sort of person who thinks ahead about my life in that way. I don't over-analyse my options. If I look back now and think about myself as a 14-year-old kid doing music and performing in local productions, I never for one second took it so seriously that I thought I absolutely *had* to make it. I was just performing because I enjoyed it. To be honest, I loved it.

One thing I definitely had, though, was persistence. I suppose I get that from my mum, who always encouraged me to do what I wanted. She'd always say, 'Louis, just go for it, give it your best shot!' My mum's very ambitious, to be fair, and I do get a lot of qualities from her. I started noticing how things worked out well if I really pushed hard, so it became kind of a self-fulfilling way of approaching my life. Once I set my mind on something I'm very stubborn and really want to achieve that goal. I've proved to myself in so many instances in life that persistence is very important, and I also think that's a big part of our success in One Direction.

Back in Doncaster, I enjoyed my time in a small band, as well as at music college and the various productions I'd been involved in locally, plus I'd picked up a few small parts in TV shows like *Fat Friends* and *Waterloo Road*, all of which really encouraged me to keep going. Each time I had some small success it would make me even more persistent, just adding fuel to the fire. I used to say, 'I just love performing, Mum. I want to just keep doing this as much as I can.' I was really enjoying being on stage – I was passionate about it and saw that world as an opportunity to get myself noticed outside of my local area.

That was my thinking behind the decision to go for *The X Factor*. As you probably know, I failed to get past the first producers' audition on my first attempt in 2009, but to be honest that rejection just made me even more determined to push on. When I went back the following year I was ready to give it everything. The previous year's disappointment was completely forgotten and if anything just motivated me more. Obviously you queue for hours for that show and while you do you get talking to people, some of whom would ask me why I was entering. I'd always reply, 'I want to get an opinion from Simon, I want to know what he thinks of my voice, what he thinks of me and whether he thinks I have something.' Once I was through the initial producers' auditions, I'd hear what he had to say about me – a genuinely weighty opinion as to whether I had anything worth pursuing.

For me that whole *X Factor* ride just went so fast. It was an amazing experience but because it was also such a blur, when you look back and reflect on those times it kinda feels like it's hard to do it justice because so much happened in such a small stretch of time. That entire phase of my life was just the most incredible period. When I try and think back to the house and all the things that went on, I can recall some of those moments but I know I've forgotten loads more! If I had a kid who fancied having a go at *The X Factor*, I'd definitely recommend that show because there's nothing else out there that offers people that kind of an opportunity. I was just a kid from a little school. I took my chance – and here I am. So, if it can happen to me . . .

zayn and Louis hour!

Mind you, I'll be totally honest, there were times during *The X Factor* when I didn't feel so positive. Obviously, the show is pre-recorded weeks in advance so I'd been telling all my friends that I'd made it through to the live part of the show in this new band. The problem was that week after week of the auditions went by – and I was nowhere to be seen! I could tell that people were beginning to think I was just messing about. Then finally, in the last week at Manchester, they showed Harry. I thought, *At last! Here I go!* But they didn't show me at all. I was really embarrassed and just assumed that everyone would think I was a time-waster. Some of my mates had previously booked a holiday to Magaluf and they'd been taking the mickey out of me for going to Boot Camp rather than going on holiday. I didn't mind that 'cos they were just messing about, really.

Then, during Boot Camp, they hardly showed me again, at least not until the band was put together. Even at that point I was watching the show and wondering, *Everyone will be thinking, 'Who is this kid that has just popped up outta nowhere with his hat on?'* So that was a weird time, being so excited knowing that I was in One Direction but contrasting that with hardly being seen on the show at all and worrying what people would be thinking.

If I thought the early shows were nerve-wracking, they were nothing compared with the extremes of emotion I felt when I was rejected from the Boys category and then suddenly put back into the competition in this band. I've spoken about that important moment in my life many times, obviously, but what I'll add is that the rejection and then the second chance was exactly the sort of opportunity that my persistent nature craved. That was a fantastic offer that I fully intended to grab with both hands. It was so exciting, that second chance, so I knew that I had to persist – keep trying my best, keep having a go, as my mum would say. I was determined to put absolutely everything into this unexpected shot they'd given me.

The X Factor is an overwhelming experience, and we were all young lads trying to soak up what was happening to us. So it really helped that there was such an immediate chemistry between the five of us. The environment on that show is so intense that I don't think the band would have worked if we'd been struggling to get on. But we just clicked, just like that. When we all hung out at Harry's step-dad's bungalow that was definitely a time when One Direction began to form this bond – this closeness – that we still enjoy today. Straight away I was pretty impressed with how we were all just chatting to each other so naturally, because we'd literally shared maybe ten conversations with each other before we came to the bungalow. We stayed there a few days, and it was just like staying with your mates from back home. We were playing PlayStation, messing about, watching TV – just having a great laugh. I'd be seeing all this kicking off and laughing so much, and all the time I just had a feeling there was something there. I don't know that I'd call it a spark, but there was definitely something there ...

Perhaps not surprisingly, I clearly remember signing our record deal. After the show had finished we went into Syco's office for the first time but it was different to how I'd imagined. I'm not sure what I expected, to be fair. Maybe something more crazy and 'showbiz', I guess, but it was just a really nice

Louis

office. Mind you, it was still pretty cool. There were gold discs of all these amazing artists on the walls, so it wasn't exactly drab! I was like, 'Look at this, lads! They did that album … and that one!' It was just hit records everywhere.

We walked in all wide-eyed and had this meeting, signed the deal and then left pretty soon after. It wasn't really until later on that I appreciated precisely how HUGE that moment was in my life. One Direction is very much like that most of the time – because everything's been so frantic for us from day one, with so many massive, mad moments, I find I have to really zone in to think about something in particular.

Recording our début album was very interesting because it was an experience filled with 'firsts' for some of us. For a start, even flying to various countries was something that not all of us had done. I'd been on a plane when I was four, but mostly I'd only ever been to France on holiday every other year – and even then we used to get the ferry over. I'd never been anywhere like LA. It was a world away from my home, obviously. A few of my mates had been to Disney World in Florida, but we never did that when I was a kid. So you can imagine that LA was a bit of a culture shock for a 19-year-old lad from Doncaster.

It was absolutely amazing, a blessing, and I felt really privileged to be there. Our hotel was more glamorous than anything I'd ever stayed in, and I was so excited to think that if everything went well there could be more of this. I said to all the lads at various points, 'If the band goes well and we work really hard, this might be a taste of things to come for us.' Despite all the craziness around us at the time and the difficulty I sometimes have in remembering specific events, I clearly remember feeling conscious of always working hard, seizing this opportunity that had been given to us.

LA was crazy, but not as nuts as when we landed back at Heathrow. Luckily for us, really early on in our career we'd seen fans outside studios and hotels, maybe a hundred or sometimes even two hundred, so we were kinda expecting a few faces at the airport. But what greeted us was just this mass of people, a sea of fans going completely mad. I was like, 'Jeez, is this for real?' We'd not seen anything like that before and the fact it was in England made it feel all the more special. I remember I got my hoody sleeve ripped clean off, so I just dumped it and I told myself, *Keep running!* Then these police officers said, 'Lads, over here, get in here!' and we were dragged into a tiny office, but all these fans were surrounding it and banging on the walls and windows. It was so intense.

Eventually, we made our get-away and once we'd got out of there and were sitting in this police van, we just sat there looking at each other. You could see we were all shell-shocked – our faces were just saying, 'What the hell just happened there, lads?' Looking back, that was the first sign that the hysteria could get seriously out of control. It was a real shock to the system.

Those early recording sessions were a time of strange contrast as well, though. I'm generally a very confident person and enjoy feeling positive about experiences. So it might surprise you to hear that away from the incredibly exciting events that were sweeping over the band seemingly every day – or at times every hour – I was actually struggling with issues of self-confidence. Like I say, that might seem a bit of an odd

Look what the tour crew are rolling in...

thing to say for someone who's known for having bagfuls of confidence – which I do have, I admit – but I'm just being honest with you. Let me explain.

For the whole of *The X Factor* I didn't have a solo. As you know, I like being the centre of attention – I don't mind admitting that. So being on the ultimate fringe was a tough pill for someone who likes the limelight to swallow at first. During the show we'd do a performance and then stand in front of the judges. They'd be saying all this stuff about our vocals or whatever, but I'd just be listening to Cheryl or Simon or whoever and thinking, *That isn't really directed at me anyway, is it?*

When we got to the recording sessions for the first album that situation deteriorated, to be honest. Obviously, the début sessions in LA and Sweden were exciting and also very challenging. I'd never been in a recording studio before, so when we got there it was massively intimidating. I was less confident about my vocal ability than some of the other lads in the band. In fact, at times I was terrified and didn't have any confidence at all. It's such a random thing: you enter a booth with these high-profile producers who you've never met before and they're like, 'Okay, Louis, sing!' Normally, I'd be a little apprehensive, but my confidence would pull me through and I'd just have a go. But there was something deeper going on behind those nerves.

I'm being really frank and honest with you here. That period was actually really tough. I was clearly delighted to be in the band and have this amazing opportunity, but at the same time I was struggling. It took me a while to find my place in One Direction. In fact, to begin with, I couldn't really understand why I was even in the band. That really ate me up at the start. Big time. I can say that was easily the hardest single period for me in One Direction. That was a real low – that feeling of not having a purpose, of just being taken along for the ride without really being a part of it. I did feel really isolated and vulnerable.

In the end I decided to do what I knew had worked in the past – be persistent. I was determined to keep working hard, carry on contributing and just ensure that I made myself absolutely essential to the creative and commercial success of the band. It probably wasn't until the recording sessions for the second album that I really started to feel comfortable with my vocals. The lads were massively helpful too, they would always boost my confidence, encourage me and just back me all the way. 'Nice one, Louis, that was wicked, your voice was amazing on that song . . .' all that kind of stuff. That helped enormously.

Looking back on that early phase, having to question myself like that has ultimately helped me because it made me work harder and prove I deserved to be in this band. Those self-doubts made me practise my vocals more and more, and pushed me to stand up and be counted. I feel lucky to have experienced that difficult phase and worked my way through it. Now I still work hard and enjoy making a big contribution to the success of the band.

Before you feel too sorry for me, though – honestly! – let me tell you that aside from my self-doubts about the vocal situation, those very early days in the band were just the most insane period. We had all these PAs and small club gigs,

293

then the *X Factor* tour – it really was a whirlwind. Getting to know the lads, being bombarded by all this stuff we had to do every day, it was so exciting!

It just kept getting madder and madder and madder. We had our début single 'What Makes You Beautiful' played on Radio 1, which was nuts, especially when we heard it played again on our car stereo on the way home from the radio station. I vividly remember sitting in the car just shaking my head, going, 'That is on Radio 1, lads. Radio 1! This is insane!' Although that song feels like a million years ago now and its lyrics represent a very different phase of our lives – we were only 17 to 19 years old at that point, remember – I stand by that record; it's still a very good pop song. Melodically it's very catchy, and the lyrics seemed to strike a chord with our fans. I think it just felt authentic, not too manufactured, even though we didn't really have much creative input on the record itself. That isn't the point – 'What Makes You Beautiful' really was the start for us. When it went straight into the charts at Number 1 we knew we were in for a mad ride ahead.

From then on it just took off even more quickly and absolutely massively. Of course, I'd like to think we worked hard and played our part – that exciting first series of PAs and all that early promo didn't do themselves – but I also have to acknowledge the role of social media in what went on. There's no doubt that without that our career would be nowhere near where it is now. Social media gave us a massive head start. We get mentioned alongside some pretty amazing names in the music business because of the success we've enjoyed, and we've worked really hard for that, for sure. At the same time, I can see how much harder it must

Louis

have been for bands like The Beatles to go out and physically promote themselves by gigging all over the world without people passing on the word through social media.

You clearly have to back up the buzz about the band on social media and we chose to do that by gigging – and gigging *hard*. You can only get so far with Twitter, Facebook, Instagram and the like. You have to gig, graft and do the interviews too. You've got to get people to know you, understand you and like you. And you've got to keep the ball rolling, because pop in particular is a very fickle business. There's always that chance that another boy band is just around the corner, so we all decided to work really hard to make sure we stayed on top. I used to talk with the lads about this when we occasionally had a brief moment to catch our breath. I'd say, 'We've just gotta keep working at it, lads, this is our chance, we have to keep going.' They all felt exactly the same.

Maybe that's something we've all picked up during our childhoods. I'm not sure we ever thought about it so consciously – we'd been asked to work hard and make something of this band, and we left no stone unturned doing just that. We knew we were incredibly lucky, so we felt we owed it to the process to really go for it. I always thought you can't just be given this opportunity and not work incredibly hard. It's such a huge thing and there are so many other people out there who would give it 100 per cent.

For example, we did a fan game called 'Bring 1D To Me', which culminated in us visiting four European countries in four days. That's just nuts, but why wouldn't you be excited about that? We were all like, 'Let's get on with it! Let's crack on!' Besides, it didn't really feel like it was work. Sure, we

'I VIVIDLY REMEMBER SITTING IN THE CAR JUST SHAKING MY HEAD, GOING, "THAT'S ON RADIO 1, LADS. RADIO 1!"'

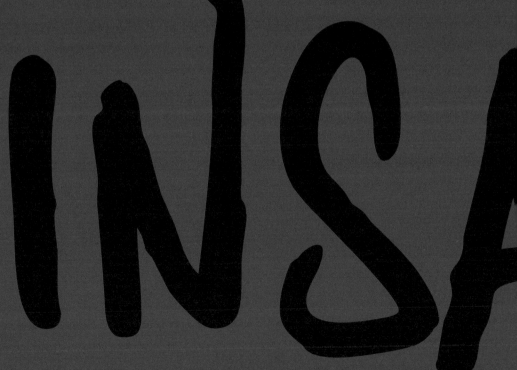

were putting in some seriously long hours, but at that point all we were essentially doing in promo and interviews was being ourselves, so it wasn't exactly a chore. A few times on the early press jaunts I could see something going on when we all walked into a room. It was fun, we had a laugh and the press people seemed to enjoy it too. There were several occasions when I sat in interviews listening to the boys crack jokes and bounce off each other, and I could see why people found that endearing and enjoyable. It was clear that we all had our part to play individually, and also that together we were somehow greater than the sum of our parts.

The culmination of all this promo and gigging was when our début album went to Number 2 in the UK and Number 1 in 17 countries. That was just mad. For me, I'd only really thought about how we might do in the UK – my home country, and where I was looking to succeed. Overseas hadn't really come into my mind, even though we'd done these press trips. Looking back, this was the first time we sensed that something was going on worldwide. It was a major wake-up call, as I suddenly saw that the band's potential might be off the scale. I, for one, hadn't even thought about that.

You could say that was naïve, and I wouldn't argue with you. I think we were all naïve at that stage, to be honest. We were just going with the flow. Someone would say, 'You're going to do four European countries in four days,' and we'd be like, 'Wey-hey, sounds crazy! Let's go!' Then they'd say, 'Right, the album's Number 1 all over the place. We need to hit the road,' and we were like, 'Great! Where's the tour bus? Let's pile in and go again!' I can see that we had an energy about us that was infectious and certainly pretty lively!

Haircut time...

The first tour in the UK was brilliant. It was a clever decision to go with theatres, not arenas. We wanted to experience a relatively normal progression, and we needed to learn. Yes, we'd done the *X Factor* tour and that had played in some arenas – which had given us a feel for that larger scale – but we were only doing four songs each night then, so now we definitely needed the theatre tour to find our feet and build our confidence. Jumping into arenas would have been stupid. We would have learnt, I guess, but I think a theatre tour first was the perfect way to go about it.

We had such a laugh on that first tour, and every night it got more and more intense. We were constantly saying, 'The fans are just unreal!' We've been so lucky to have had such an amazing following from day one – and now, all this time later, they're still with us. Back then, so much was going on every day it would've been easy to get overwhelmed, but as I mentioned before, I always try not to think too much about things. I don't see the point in over-analysing situations.

I'll tell you what did make a huge difference to my enjoyment of this fantastic time, though – the other four lads. I feel so much less pressure when I have them around to talk to, bounce ideas off and just muck about with. The dynamic in the band seemed to find a level very quickly – we all somehow knew if one of us needed a bit of picking up, or maybe if someone just could do with some space for a while. Looking back, that's pretty cool because we were only young. Then, as now, I certainly enjoyed having that banter and camaraderie around me. I often wonder how solo artists deal with life on the road. I always say on tour, 'I've no idea how solo artists cope. It's beyond me!'

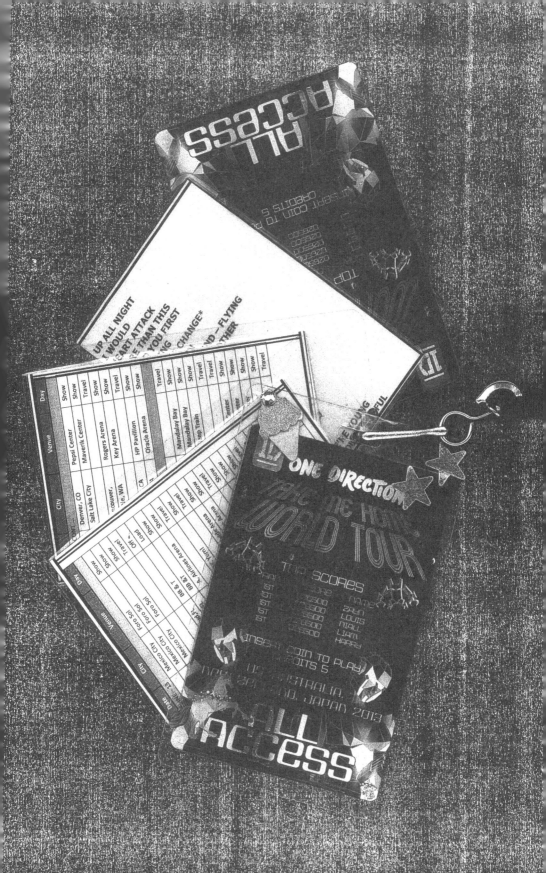

If we thought those early days in the UK were crazy, they were really nothing – just the calm before the storm – compared with when it kicked off in the States. We signed the US record deal around the same time as our début single came out in the UK, and we then had to wait till February for our first tour over there, supporting Big Time Rush.

Even though in the UK the band was attracting a lot of attention, our expectations in the US were much more modest. Our social media following was big by this point, but this didn't necessarily guarantee anything. Or so we thought. There was a lot of discussion before the Big Time Rush tour of managing our expectations, of not getting carried away. Before those first shows in the States we'd had a solid talk from management. They said, 'Look, it's not your show. This isn't the UK. Most of the people will be there for Big Time Rush and they won't know any of your songs. They might know the singles, but just be prepared for a pretty muted reception. You need to be realistic.'

Well, we went out on stage on the first night as the support band and the place went *completely* mental. At various points during the show, I'd wander over to each of the lads in turn and say, 'Can you believe what's happening here?' We were all just bewildered. The reception was just ten times better than we could ever have imagined. No, a hundred times better! It was an amazing reaction. It was also a bit awkward because we were on that tour as guests of Big Time Rush – and they were great guys. They worked really hard and were really lovely to all of us, total gentlemen.

After the first couple of nights went so well, I said to the lads, 'Maybe every single fan from every corner of the US has somehow managed to get tickets to the first two shows?' But by the third, fourth, fifth night that this mad crowd reaction was happening, it started to dawn on us that every night was going to be completely bonkers. That's when I started to get the feeling, *Hey, maybe this could work in America too?* And there were other signs that something was possibly going on in the States for us. 'What Makes You Beautiful' hit the Top 30, which was great, although, to be fair, pop bands can often have a decent single out in the US only to see their album sink without trace. So we enjoyed the reception we were getting but just kept our foot to the floor. We'd say, 'Work, work, work. Take nothing for granted. Don't stop.'

The momentum behind One Direction was starting to feel massive. I know I've said we were all pretty naïve about the situation, and that's true, but there were certain pivotal points when it was possible for us to step back and think, *This is totally nuts!* The performance on the *Today* show during the week of the début album's release was one such moment. That was such a massive, televised indication of the buzz surrounding the band. We were starting to think that things were going reasonably well in the States, but then we did that show – and BOOM!

To this day I still think that's probably one of the best performances we've ever done. It was surreal to be in New York, surrounded by this vast sea of faces, all those towering buildings and the total hysteria. It was insane. It was certainly very difficult to take on board what was going on, but I think we did a good job with the actual performance. When that many people come to see the band you just can't comprehend the scale of the crowd. Before the show, one of the presenters

'WE'D SAY, "WORK, WORK, WORK. TAKE NOTHING FOR GRANTED. DON'T STOP.

DON't" STOP".

had said something like, 'We had an inkling that this morning's concert would be a big draw,' and he wasn't wrong! There were thousands and thousands of fans there. You see the first 200 people – and after that it becomes quite hard to even focus on anything else. I like to try to zone in on people as far back as I can see. They've made all that effort to come to see you, so I want to try to include everyone in the show. The people right at the back have just as much right to feel involved as the fans up at the front, and if I can do that in some small way I will. At the *Today* show, those streets of New York were just heaving. It was such a buzz. After we'd left the venue we watched the footage back, and it was only then, I think, that we were fully able to realise the true scale of what we'd just seen. What a day!

When we woke up the next morning we just pushed on again. There was never a sense of holding anything back. We wanted to work, we were hungry for success, and the more they threw at us the more we wanted it. In a way, considering this was relatively early days for the band, we were still quite a unit, and I think our naïvety was a strength.

I suppose the moment when we all had to acknowledge that something big was happening was when the album went to Number 1 in the US charts. Then it was cemented: 'Right, lads, we've done OK in the US'. Initially, we'd chatted about the prospects for the album and had said, 'A Top Twenty record would be happy days!' Then we got the pre-orders in, which were pretty huge, so that ramped up expectations, I'm not gonna lie. Then the midweek sales figures came in during the week of release and suddenly I was like, 'We're actually in with a chance to get Number 1 here, lads.' That was like a red rag to a bull for us, so we just upped the workload even more, literally filling every waking second with promo. It was like we were on a mission.

Even so, when we heard we'd got the top spot it was a pretty surreal experience. Then to hear all the crazy history behind what that achievement actually meant really made us sit up and think about what we'd done. I knew about The Beatles, but all those silly comparisons to them still annoy me because they were far too good and far too cool compared to One Direction. I was like, 'Come on, let's get realistic!' Hearing people talk about The Beatles is ridiculous. Of course you can't compare us to them – on any level, in my opinion. I've far too much respect for that band and music history to get carried away with comparisons like that.

Commercially, I could see that we'd achieved something special, though – unique, as it turned out – for a British band. We were only teenagers at the time, remember, and less than two years ago we'd all been standing in a line, queueing for a TV talent show. So when you hear all these statistics about breaking records, it's like they almost can't sink in properly. *No other UK band had ever débuted at Number 1 in the States.* None. So it was quite odd when people were name-checking us in the same breath as all these legendary acts, to be honest.

It's a weird one, 'cos you feel dead proud – so we should, to be fair – but there's a feeling of . . . I won't say guilt, because we'd worked very hard. But it was an odd feeling. I don't know, maybe that sounds too harsh on us. We made that Number 1 happen – we did the graft, we made the record, so we deserved that moment. And let's face it, that

Louis

308

was a big moment. From then on, the rest of the year was a blur. One big, crazy, fantastic blur.

I'm often asked how I processed what was going on at this point. Like I said, we were less than 18 months out of *The X Factor*, and now thousands of people were screaming at us in a street in New York. I could give you some rubbish about sitting back and reflecting calmly, putting it all in perspective and understanding the context. But the simple, honest answer is that you just go with it. You can't really comprehend it all. It's almost like you have got this shield up, and no matter what people tell you and how amazing the events around you are, you're really just kinda caught up in the bubble. You go with the ride and it's all you can do to take one day at a time. Literally, that's what I used to say – 'OK, let's do today. Then let's work through tomorrow. One day at a time.'

With the album at Number 1 in the States, the workload just went through the roof, which was never more apparent than with the North American and Australian tour that year. That was a very tiring two months, but WOW! What an amazing experience. Sure, there were times when one or more of us were tired, missing home or feeling deflated. But that would never last long. The rest of the lads would always be there to pick them up and make them laugh again. We'd become a pretty tight unit by this point. I loved that tour.

That summer we also did the Olympics, which really was a privilege. I mainly remember an overwhelming sense of honour. I always think it's amazing doing what we do in One Direction, but as a football fan I think pulling on an England shirt to compete for your country must also be incredible. It's got to be the best feeling, and by singing at the Olympics it almost felt a little bit like we were doing that – representing Great Britain. It was just a real honour.

Like a lot of the band's big moments, the Olympics closing ceremony just went so quick. We did a soundcheck the day before, then we turned up about lunchtime on the day itself, proper excited. We were just hanging around, and me and Liam were bored so we said, 'We're in the Olympic Stadium, so let's go and have a look around!' We snuck out and decided to just do weird missions to annoy our tour manager, Paul, who's a worrier. We took photos of ourselves at all these points around the stadium and backstage area where we shouldn't have really been, texting him shots of us messing about. We managed to sneak into the water polo without tickets, watched a bit of that, and we even came back with someone else's clothing, as this woman who worked at Mercedes gave us her hat and jacket. Stupid and immature? Absolutely!

When you're invited to perform at the Olympics you're of course aware that someone out there considers you to be a recognised face, or at least a band with a following. That's undeniable, but I still can't see how we qualified. I'd never want to be a celebrity. In my eyes, being famous and being a celebrity are two completely different things, and personally I don't want anything to do with being called a celebrity. You have to have a purpose – you need to be respected for what you do, not what parties you go to. I don't really meet that many celebrities, funnily enough. And those celebrity parties can be so fake. There's this weird vibe when you go to them where everyone thinks they have to automatically be friends

Louis

louis

thanks America for
a great tour!!!

just because they're all famous. I just cringe at the whole thing. I've just tried to remain – we all have – as normal as possible within the confines of doing what I recognise is an unusual job. You cannot let the fame game change you.

Awards ceremonies always give you strange glimpses of this celebrity culture. I never really feel comfortable going to them, to be honest. We've been thrown into some pretty high-profile ones, even early on. For example, the first time we went to the VMAs I was like, 'I've never heard of them.' Nor had Zayn. That seems crazy now, but I'm just being honest. It was another one of those big One Direction moments, in September 2012, when we won three awards. But a lot of the awards nights are just big corporate events full of executives and famous people admiring themselves. There's not really much conversation, you just kinda glance over to everyone, give the odd nod of recognition. It all just feels quite surreal. We went to one awards ceremony in 2013 and Rihanna was literally right in front of us. We were well impressed! We were like, 'Hey, look, lads. There's Rihanna!' It's not that we feel we don't deserve to be there, but we still have that sense of five lads being a little bit out of place, like the new kids at school. Someone said to me that maybe Rihanna was looking over at us lot, but I doubt that!

We did get a few jeers at the early awards ceremonies, but more recently there's been a sense that we've earned people's respect by the work we've put in to achieve our success. I understand that some people don't like *The X Factor*, where we started, but I'll never talk that show down to win doubters round. I love *The X Factor* and I wouldn't say a bad word about it. I think it's a great show and a great platform.

315

Getting back to the subject of celebrities, we've been lucky enough to meet some really cool famous people. I find the more famous someone is, the more grounded they usually are. Perhaps they've been around long enough to get used to the pitfalls and have come out the other side. A really great example is Johnny Depp. We'd heard his kids were fans of the band, which was cool. Originally he was going to come down to a show with his family, but he had an injury of some kind and was on crutches, so he said, 'I can't make it. So why don't you come down to my house and meet the kids?' We were like, 'Er, OK. Let's all pile round Johnny Depp's house. Great!' So we did, and that was a great experience. I took my mate Olly, and he couldn't believe it! Parents will do anything for their kids, and I'm glad Johnny Depp did. What a legend!

As a massive footy obsessive I've got to mention David Beckham too. He's the only person that I'd stand in a queue for days to see. People ask about which bands I'd line up to meet, but none come anywhere near Beckham for me. He's such an icon, and for me, as a kid growing up in Doncaster playing football, I just thought he was incredible. Still do.

Anyway, get this, right. The first time he was around the band no one told me and I missed him altogether! I went bonkers and was proper gutted. There were some crossed wires where various crew members thought someone else had told me he was about, but in the end I completely missed him. I heard he was about so I asked where, and one of the crew said, 'Oh, sorry, Louis, he's gone now, mate.' I was gutted. 'Are you taking the mick? David Beckham was here and I was just sat in the trailer on the PlayStation?' Fortunately, we later got invited to the film première for *Class of*

'92, produced by our friend Ben Winston, and David Beckham was there again. This time I got to meet him and he was lovely. I thought about trying to play it cool, but it's so hard around someone like that. So in the end I just kept fairly quiet. Fair play to him. He always carries himself with such style, and I hear he's made a few dollars! I just look at him and can't do anything but admire how he handles himself. I think he must be wired up differently to me because I wouldn't be able to be in the public eye for over 20 years.

Back on Planet One Direction we were doing stacks of gigs, promoting ourselves constantly and getting ready to release the second album. I was feeling far more comfortable with my own vocals, as those early problems I'd had on the first album had largely faded away.

This time we'd become more involved in the writing of the album. We did a week in Sweden and were starting to feel a bit more part of the creative process, but again it was only really lyrics at that stage. That was cool. I think the success we'd had so far gave us the confidence to speak up in writing sessions a bit more. On the first album we weren't ready, but by now there was a growing feeling of wanting to have more input. I'd say, 'Maybe we can try this lyric like this?' or 'How about we change that around and sing it like this?' Just ideas, suggestions, alternatives really. That said, we didn't really push it too hard because we did still feel quite inexperienced. We didn't feel ready yet – and it was definitely the right thing to be cautious. Take it at a steady pace.

Second time round there was a pretty massive change of expectation – the first album obviously had nothing to live up

317

to, whereas now we were following up a record that had quite literally gone around the world. On the first album, people had been saying, 'This could be Number 1,' but suddenly that had changed to, 'So, do you think you will be Number 1 again?' That's a very different question, and it has a different impact in terms of pressure and expectations. Fortunately, the speed of our non-stop schedule stopped us procrastinating over the second record, so there was no chance to over-write or over-complicate it. We just concentrated on the songs – they were sounding cool and we were playing them to people who said they were great, but there are only so many opinions you can get. We were like, 'We just want to get the record out there and see what the fans think.' Those were the opinions we really needed.

So you can imagine how delighted we were when the new album *Take Me Home* went straight in at Number 1 in 31 countries. 31! That was a big statement, and we definitely felt the significance of that achievement. I clearly remember going online one day to look at the iTunes charts. 'Harry! Have you seen the state of these charts?!' The record was at the top of all these territories – it was just worldwide, Number 1 all over the place. What a buzz!

The month after that ludicrous chart news we did our Madison Square Garden show. What a night that was! Along the way there have been various moments that felt like they were watershed points, like we were writing our own history, creating a series of key events that would always be symbolic of what was going on for One Direction at the time. MSG was like that and, for once, we really did feel its significance at exactly the moment it happened. Before we were booked to

do the show I didn't really know about the iconic status and legend of Madison Square Garden, but in the lead-up to the gig I'd schooled myself a little on that out of respect for the venue and its history. We got there on the day and were walking around looking at all the photos of previous performers. Every one of us was like, 'This is absolutely mad!' All the legends had played there. We had a camera crew with us as well, so in many ways it was such a nervy day. But there was also a tangible, overwhelming sense of honour. It was a real privilege to play there.

Talking of privileges, what can I say about our trip to Ghana for Comic Relief? It's unquestionably one of the most amazing experiences of my life. For starters, flying to a place where no one had any idea who we were was a complete contrast to being recognised wherever we went. Most of the people we met didn't speak much English, but that didn't seem to matter. We chatted away and they were just so nice to us.

It was amazing. Once you've been out there and seen that world with your own eyes, it's so hard to come home and get across how much you should look at yourself and think, *I need to stop whinging.* One thing I noticed was that a lot of the film clips from fund-raising programmes show how terrible things are and how upset people in need can be, which is of course sadly very true and we've all got to be aware of that despair. But in their day-to-day life these people are, in many ways, so happy and positive. That was what struck me as the most incredible aspect of that trip: seeing people living in abject poverty, where the stench of faeces was unbelievable, and yet you've got all these smiling kids playing football and laughing and enjoying themselves. You've got little boys walking round in girls' T-shirts 'cos it's all stuff from charities, but they're laughing and playing. Everybody says hello to everyone else, everyone waves and smiles.

It was an incredible trip. As soon as we got back I said to my girlfriend, 'I've got to take you out there one day because I think it would be such a great experience.' For anyone, in fact. I was genuinely sad when we left because those people were so cool. They totally blew me away, and their attitude in the face of such poverty was pretty incredible. They have this real sense of community, which, in a way, is all they've got.

By sharp contrast, in the same month we started our headline world tour, our longest-ever live jaunt. That was crazy, a huge stint on the road. We knew we were going away for a long time, which was a little bit daunting but so exciting too. We started in the O2, which was crazy − thanks for the easy start, management! − and we also filmed these shows for our forthcoming movie. So it was a really nervy start.

It definitely can get monotonous in the back of a bus or in another hotel room when you've just played your 60th show and you're not even halfway through the tour. Fortunately, we took a few chances to go home, but we didn't mind being away for so long on such a big tour. This was our opportunity to really get out there and show the world what we could do on stage. Strip it all back, and that's what rock 'n' roll is all about − playing live. It's gotta be done − and we love it!

A typical day for me on the road with One Direction involves getting offstage at about half ten at night, then hanging out on the tour bus and staying up till about six in the morning, 'cos that's our only time to relax and socialise. Then I'll sleep till about two in the afternoon, then try to recharge myself before it all starts again. Usually there's a ton of promo and interviews to fit in as well. Yes, it's hard work, but I love being on the bus – it's my favourite thing. It's cool, 'cos after a show I'm on such a natural buzz from the adrenalin, so the thought of going back to a hotel room and sitting on my own . . . well, I can't think of anything worse. So we just sit on the bus, watch films, play PlayStation, kick a ball about. It's great.

Like a few of the other boys, at times I don't sleep particularly well. In any case, we work so much in the day that I can't possibly just finish up, lie down and go to sleep straight away. I need to have some social time to switch off and get my head around fun stuff. Being in the band is an all-consuming part of my life, so if I don't try to make time for other things I'd never do anything else. Luckily, I don't need a lot of sleep – four or five hours is usually enough. For me, all of this would be impossible to do on my own, and without the lads it would be no fun at all.

As for getting stage fright and nerves when I'm performing in front of these massive crowds, I feel very lucky because I don't really suffer too much from these. Normally before a show I am like, 'I can't wait! Let's get out there, lads!' If I know that family or friends are in the audience I can get quite nervous, but in the course of a normal show I usually feel OK. I don't really like to say I don't get nervous at all 'cos I think this comes across as a little arrogant, so I'd prefer to say I just really look forward to the performance. For the first five or so gigs of any tour we're all finding our way around the stage, getting used to the set and the vibe – no amount of rehearsals can prepare you for standing in front of tens of thousands

Louis

Don't the guys
look great?

of people – but once we settle into the whole show it's just the best adrenalin rush, night after night. By then I don't feel the nerves because the adrenalin takes over. I'm in the zone, and because you know the show inside out by then it's just a total pleasure. And, of course, with One Direction fans being so loud, so crazy and so supportive, how can we not love being on tour and meeting them every night?

In my opinion, part of the appeal of a One Direction show is that we kinda fly by the seat of our pants. In fact, we've always done so, up to a point. Clearly, in the past you've had pop shows where the band has to be 100 per cent rehearsed, and dancing that has to be on point and perfect. But with us we mess up, forget the lyrics, laugh it off and hopefully can get away with that kind of stuff. The crowd laugh with us, and that does take the pressure off a little bit.

It was during the *Take Me Home* tour that much of the footage for our movie *This Is Us* was shot. What an amazing opportunity for the band to have a movie made like that. The cameras followed us for a long time, but we're used to all that, to be honest. We started off on a TV show, after all! For the most part the filming for *The X Factor* tries to keep things relatively natural, so we were allowed to be ourselves around the cameras.

That early experience taught us well. Fast-forward to our second album tour and here we are again, with cameras following pretty much our every waking moment. Don't get me wrong, there are some days when it's definitely tiresome having cameras in our faces – occasionally you just want a day when you don't have to mike up. But that's just the odd day, and mainly we love it.

We also all felt it was such a great opportunity to document what we're doing with One Direction in real detail. That might be a selfish way to look at it, but that movie will be a really nice film to look back on in 30 years. It tells our story. To a certain extent it also allowed us a rare chance to look outside of the One Direction bubble, to see the crowds, the fans outside, the gigs. I remember saying to the lads, 'It feels kinda cool that we actually get to watch our own show for once.'

The movie première was a real laugh too! That was a big deal, and the huge crowd in Leicester Square was amazing. I remember saying to Niall, 'Mate, this is just the best, can you believe how far this band has come, this is Leicester Square!' It was a very proud day for us – all our families came, my mum, my little sisters, my girlfriend. Me and Niall messed about in the cinema and kept getting annoyed glances from people, but it was our movie so we were allowed to!

Funnily enough, I found the seven-hour online broadcast for 1D Day more stressful than turning up at that huge film première. It was definitely one of the most stressful days that we've had, but it was great at the same time. We've never presented anything on live TV before and I can tell you it's a really hard thing to do, especially for so many hours. You kinda take it for granted when you see people on TV do it, so I've nothing but admiration for them now! We had a few technical difficulties, like when me and Niall tried to get through to Doctor Who and it just didn't work, which was awkward. Also, the autocue kept going off, which meant we had to ad-lib lots of stuff to keep it going. But all in all it was a great day and a big achievement. I think we put on a good show in the end and I really enjoyed it.

Louis

By the autumn of 2013 we'd enjoyed so much success it was hard to imagine how our next album could keep up with what had gone before. Well, *Midnight Memories* charted at the top in 31 countries around the world. I really cannot comprehend that ... I'm crap at geography, so I certainly can't even name 31 countries off the top of my head. To then think of all those people going out and buying or downloading the record in that first week in all those places is frankly just mind-boggling. Once again I went on iTunes for the charts. 'Harry, mate, it's time to look at those charts again ...' It was ridiculous. It seemed to be Number 1 on virtually every list. That was sick.

With all three of our albums going straight in at Number 1 in the States too, that was another crazy new One Direction record. I actually feel guilty that we'll never be able to get out and play shows in all of those countries, but we're so grateful to every single fan who bought that record. Having done so much of the writing on the third album meant that it really mattered to us what people thought about the record. And to have it sell so strongly was a fantastic feeling.

There are obvious benefits to being in a successful band like One Direction. Clearly, we're lucky enough to be able to buy nice houses and cars and all those sorts of things. What young lad wouldn't enjoy that part of it?! In the early days there were occasions when it showed me who my real friends were, in the sense that a few people made jealous or nasty comments. Throughout the whole experience I've kinda kept about ten proper mates from way back when I was a kid. I guess that's a pretty healthy number of people to have who

I really trust and know have my best interests at heart. The whole One Direction experience has been an amazing one for my family. They've never been anything other than incredibly supportive – they constantly champion what I'm doing and have never once faltered in backing me all the way. For that I'm very grateful.

We do need to keep an eye on enjoying our private time because otherwise we'd do nothing else apart from One Direction! At the start of 2014 we had a three-month break, which was fantastic. It was a real chance to finally recharge a little. During those three months most of my time was taken up with football, training at Doncaster Rovers, who for some strange reason signed me on a professional contract! I've got a shirt number and everything now: number 28. I trained hard for four weeks and was then asked to play for the reserves in a full-on professional game. On the night of the match I was much, much more nervous than I've ever been for a One Direction show. The only thing I can compare that experience to is my first audition for *The X Factor*. People ask me why I was so nervous – after all I perform in front of thousands of people in the band – but it's not the same. I'm an amateur footballer, and back then I was an amateur singer and so I absolutely crapped myself! In that game I felt like everyone was looking at me. Let's face it, there were ten professional footballers out there – and then me. We drew nil–nil. I did alright, I think.

It's really exciting for me to be involved in that football club because it feels like the start of One Direction again. I'm really intrigued by the whole football world: sitting in with the gaffer on transfer deadline day in January, really getting a feel

for what professional football is like. They're putting me on the board of directors, so I'll keep heavily involved and continue supporting the club as much as I can. On one of the screens for the 2014 stadium tour I'm even wearing my Doncaster Rovers shirt – anything I can do to help promote the club! I'm on the back of the programme every week, I've a real passion for it and I really look forward to doing more and more with the club.

Away from football I also went on a songwriting trip to LA with Liam, and spent some time with my girlfriend and our dog. Just doing really nice, normal stuff.

When we do get some rare time off, it's a pretty mad dash to get round to see all my family and friends! We might only have, say, three days off, so I bomb off up to Doncaster and get to see my family, my mum, grandma, sisters and mates. It can be almost as tiring as being on tour! It's always fantastic to catch up with people in person, though, so whenever possible I try to do that. Balancing your time can be hard in a band that's as busy as One Direction, but I try my best.

I do notice that even during my time off I think about the band pretty much constantly. I know I've said I don't overthink things and just try to enjoy the moment, but on occasion I know I can be very self-critical. Not to such an extent that it eats me up, but I can criticise myself quite readily. That implies a level of self-analysis, of reflecting on events and how well or badly I've done. It's not often that I get the breathing space to do that in One Direction, but if I do I'll usually find something that I want to improve on, do better, try differently. I think this is healthy and all part of being ambitious and proud of what I do. I can be a perfectionist – and at times

that's difficult – but I just fall back on that persistence I had as a kid. And just keep grafting, grafting, grafting.

At times life in One Direction can be exhausting. It's easy to feel overwhelmed, to make mistakes or do something daft that you later regret. The schedules are pretty demanding too. But you know what? It's all worth it – every day, every hour, every minute, every second. How can we not enjoy it, how can I not be grateful for the opportunity and the privilege of all the amazing experiences that I've had?

Before I got into One Direction my general perception of celebrities and bands was that their lives were a piece of cake, easy work. That's the way a lot of people think. 'Money for nothing' and so on. Well, now I'm on the other side of that misconception I can tell you it's a lot of hard work. There are obvious downsides, such as the loss of privacy and all that, but that's a small price to pay for the privilege of being in One Direction. You have to keep that perspective. It's a tough world out there for a lot of people who work incredibly hard and maybe don't get paid much or don't have the opportunity to travel or experience much of life. So whatever tough times we're having professionally need to be judged in that context.

I still think the best way forward isn't to analyse too much what has happened, but just keep enjoying each moment. So I personally try to stay away from thinking too deeply about things, because how can you fully comprehend what this band has achieved? If I did switch my phone off and sit down to reflect on everything that has happened to us, it would just be completely mind-blowing.

It's great to be so busy and doing something creative. At my age that's cool. If I hadn't gone to that audition, I would

probably not have made it to uni, in which case I'd have more than likely just bummed around a bit. Now, I think, I can say I've achieved something.

You do hear of bands running out of steam, burning out with the schedules and demands of being a high-profile group. For me, personally, I have as much fire in my belly for this band now as I've ever had – certainly as much as when I stood in that queue for *The X Factor* all those years ago. The minute we stop trying to get better is when we'll go into decline, but that can't be allowed to happen. We're always trying to improve, make better music and keep the progression rolling. As soon as we start to rely on what we've already achieved, we'll get bored and the fans will get bored. We can't let that happen.

If I could speak to that kid from Doncaster standing there back in 2010 waiting to impress Simon Cowell, knowing everything that I do now and having experienced this crazy life in One Direction, I'd tell him to sing his heart out ... and to get ready for the ride of his life.

Louis

'if I could speak to
that kid from Doncaster
standing there back in 2010
waiting to impress Simon
Cowell, knowing everything
that I do now and having
experienced this crazy life
in One Direction, I'd tell him
to sing his heart out . . .
and to get ready
for the ride of
his life.'

the
boys

Liam: People are always curious about what happens in One Direction when we're not at work. There are many amazing elements of being in this band, and songwriting is right up there as one of the most important and enjoyable. Along with actually performing to our fans, songwriting has become something we really enjoy. It's also another way that we get to be creative and feel like we can communicate directly with the fans.

Niall: For me it's the guitar side of music that first got me into writing songs. I started playing the guitar as a young kid, although I didn't have an immediate knack for songwriting – that wasn't my thing. It was more playing around with chords and trying to learn to play songs that I liked listening to. I did tend to enjoy playing singer-songwriters' tunes more, though. I listened to a lot of country music back then and still do. The melodies are just so strong. I love The Eagles, they're still my favourite band. Their songs have undeniably some of the best melodies ever written, and that's definitely influenced how I write.

Zayn: I was mad into the performing arts at an early age. Obviously, having roles in musicals and later discovering R&B and rap, I started to think about how these songs that I liked were created. The creative spark involved in songwriting has always fascinated me.

Liam: Do any of you lot remember the first song you wrote?

Harry: I actually have it! I was about 15 when I wrote it. Recently an old school mate sent it to me on email. It's funny to hear my voice 'cos I sound so different. There are a couple

The boys

of songs I did at school that are quite funny. One I did with the band I was in, White Eskimo, was called something like 'Luggage'. The chorus was pretty much something about going away for a week or two: 'I don't need any jackets or shoes, the only luggage I need is you!' If you hear that on a One Direction album in a few years, that was my idea ...

Liam: Ha ha, brilliant. In terms of writing for One Direction, when I first started songwriting with other people I was nervous about suggesting ideas. We were just kids starting out.

Louis: I didn't feel as involved at first because there were a lot of people in the room each time – there was a lot going on. Songwriting can be so personal, which is why I prefer the smaller sessions.

Zayn: I think 'cos I'm a bit quieter, my natural shyness meant I was initially holding back on the song ideas that were coming into my head. We couldn't shout up on the first album because we didn't feel we had the experience to do it. We didn't know how to go about writing a song.

Liam: Gradually I noticed that even some of the really successful songwriters will sometimes just mumble a few lines of a lyric, or hum a really rough melody – just to get the idea out into the open and start the process. Sometimes you'll all laugh if what they or you suggested sounds daft, but after that you play around with the idea and usually something will crop up as a result. I used to be too scared to speak up, but now I've gained confidence and really enjoy putting ideas out there.

Harry: It definitely feels more appropriate that we put our ideas forward these days. There's a bit more justification behind them, partly due to the work we've put in so far with the band and also because some of our own songs have made it onto the albums and been enjoyed at gigs too.

I now have nine little books full of lyrics and poems! It's a cool thing to be able to go into a writing session with these poems written down and put them out there to be looked at. I just say, 'Here's a few ideas. Do you think there's something here?' I love the freedom that comes with the whole process. Even if you're writing something that you really like and want on your iPod, hopefully other people will want it on theirs too.

Louis: I never really saw my current obsession with songwriting developing. I always liked the idea of writing but it kinda just happened. Generally I tend to write a lot with Liam.

Liam: Everyone is different – you have to just go with what works for you individually. Song ideas can hit you at any time – I'll be in the car driving home and think of an idea for a song and I'll hit Tommo up. I'll phone him and tell him about it, then send it over. We work like that quite a bit.

Louis: We put in a lot of extra hours to write the third album. Same with the fourth. I like the sense of achievement you feel after you've finished a song – that's amazing. Then it fuels your next writing session.

Harry: Looking back, I'm glad that we did it in the way we did, you know. We took our time and only gradually involved

The boys

ourselves in the writing process. When you listen to amazing writers, hear a great album or listen to a fantastic song on the radio, you're always learning.

Louis: Songwriting gives us five a chance to have our own creative input into the band and also to influence the musical lives of the people who support One Direction. When I listen to music and I get in the same headspace as the writer, it's really powerful – we love the idea of our fans feeling the same way. That's why it's so good to be writing on our albums. It feels like such a great sense of achievement to have a proper musical influence on the band and have that direct contact with the fans through our music.

Liam: We just don't want to stop – we want to keep working at it. We're slowly putting the pieces together as our fans grow up, so that the music grows with us all. Songwriting is something that we all absolutely love doing. On my rare days off I can't wait to get writing. Someone once said to me that songwriters wanna get up early in the morning just so they can write a song. That's bang on. You catch the bug for it! Now I'm proper addicted.

Niall: Speaking of being addicted, along with songwriting, the biggest buzz you'll ever get from this band is performing live. Way back at those first PA gigs just after *The X Factor* we were getting a massive buzz from performing. Now, as we write this book in spring 2014, we're just starting the stadium tour ... and the buzz just seems to get bigger and bigger.

the boys

Liam: Shall we mention that backstage 'incident' on the Big Time Rush tour?

ALL: Absolutely!

Liam: Something happened on the first night of the Big Time Rush tour that for me is indicative of our fans and what a phenomenon the One Direction live experience was then and still is – even more so actually. As we've mentioned elsewhere in the book, we were all quite apprehensive about our first performances in the US. We didn't expect anyone to know us or our songs, and certainly not any of the lyrics.

Niall: We weren't even allowed a soundcheck on that tour 'cos it wasn't our show, so that's the context. We had proper low expectations.

Harry: That first night we saw a load of people wearing One Direction T-shirts and started to think something was going on. Then we were all backstage after the show when the American promoter came bursting into the dressing room.

Niall: We could hear him coming down the corridor, he was so excited and loud … He was this big, larger-than-life, very flamboyant American, really loud and full of energy … but at the time we'd never met him before!

Louis: Exactly. He just came rushing in and we were all quite shocked …

Zayn: I was like, wide-eyed . . . who is this fella?

Liam: And then he said . . .

ALL: 'YOU GUYS BLOW MY FREAKIN' MIND!'

Harry: He was going, 'This is gonna be great. You guys are gonna be great!' and that shocked us a bit. I thought we were just going over to the US to have a bit of fun, and yet this guy was convinced it was gonna work.

Niall: He said, 'You're gonna be massive stars!' It turns out he'd worked with some of the biggest bands in the world. He still says he's never seen anything like it before.

Liam: It was so funny and such a shock. Remember, we'd never met him before. We didn't even know what job he did at the time! It was a huge deal because it was such an exciting reaction.

Zayn: It was hilarious, exciting and serious all at the same time. Looking back, though, what that incident highlights is the incredible power and energy of our fans. Yes, we had performed pretty well that night, we were on good form, but his reaction was really because of how our fans had reacted to us. They caused that reaction.

Louis: Don't you think it's a shame, though, that we don't get to spend more time with the fans directly? Without them we wouldn't be where we are today. The whole thing baffles me, though, and I still find it incredible how people can be so crazy about us!

Niall: Hopefully our fans still see us as the same five lads who first made it into the band back in the day. I really hope so. We always try to get out as much as we can, 'cos apart from all the amazing experiences in the band, these fans completely changed my life, and my family's life – that's how I look at it. They gave us this opportunity.

Harry: It's just very humbling. That feeling never fades, no matter how much you do this.

Liam: We all know that we wouldn't be here without the fans, like Niall says. They massively paved the way for us with all the hard work they did on Twitter. I honestly think the big marketing companies need to be looking at some of these people who have Twitter accounts and are so driven and expert. They could employ some of them. This is something they love to do every day. They sit there and make it happen, so someone should tap into that passion and that expertise and get them into an office. They'd be amazing, plus they'd get a buzz off it.

From the very first moment the fans have been there for us. I know we always say that we appreciate everything they've done for us, but we really do. We never lose sight of that. Our fans are still the best fans in the world, there's just no doubt about that.

Louis: Exactly. It's a major reason why I love the tour. That's our chance to get in the same place as the fans and have an amazing time. It strips everything away and it's just the most pure and energised experience, night after night.

Harry: We rehearse really hard for every tour because we want the shows to do them proud. When it came to tour rehearsals for our 2014 stadium shows, we headed north of London to a massive former aircraft hangar. Inside this huge building, the crew had set up the entire stage ready for rehearsals – all the screens, the pyrotechnics, everything.

Louis: It did take a while for me to actually comprehend the size of the stage and set. Wow! When you think deeply about it and remember when we started out with that small tour of Scottish clubs, then the theatre tour stage ... well, we never ever expected, or even considered, that we'd ever get to this point.

Liam: It was completely breathtaking when we first walked in and saw the set. We stood on that huge stage and I just had this overwhelming feeling. This is ours, lads. That's actually all our kit, it's so amazing and so huge! It's also quite mad to see how many people we work with now. I actually felt a bit of pressure about that, I'm not gonna pretend otherwise, but it's an absolute privilege.

Niall: When I walked in there and saw the stage, I was like, 'Woah! This is just ridiculous!' Hard to put into words, to be fair. For the 2014 tour rehearsals, we pretty much had the full tour set-up backstage. If you'd been a fly on the wall during those weeks, this is what you'd have seen. So there are a

345

couple of trailers that we can hang out in, then the mobile office where all the management and crew organisation takes place. You might wander past and see fans' cuddly toy presents on a few speaker cabinets!

Zayn: Yup, then there's a massive marquee, the best bit – catering. They do three meals a day for EVERYONE and, with a crew of about 100, that's a lot of dinners! Next to that's a smaller marquee for our clothes and where we get changed.

Louis: Outside we have a couple of motorhomes, our tour buses where we can sleep on site if we want to. They've got all the usual home comforts in there and, most importantly, the PlayStation! We sometimes have little barbecues next to the buses just to chill out.

Zayn: We have a couple of go-karts too, so when the work is over we love to blast those up and down outside, let off a bit of steam! We've also got some quad bikes, a couple of electric scooters, a table tennis table, air hockey and an arcade game – boys' toys, basically!

Louis: Most importantly of all, we have two full-size football goalposts. Yep. Essential tour equipment! Tour rehearsals can be a real laugh. We work hard in the day, but at night we have the tour bus on site to hang out in. One of the nights Liam stayed over with me and we had a bit of a wander around the hangar's site. We'd heard that in the hangar next door they do various big-budget blockbuster films, so we said, 'Let's go and have a look!' At about two in the morning

The boys

the guys
at the
Instagram
booth.

 36k   477k   👤 181

we hopped over the fence and wandered around the perimeter trying all these locked doors. We didn't think to read the signs on any of these big metal doors until Liam twigged and said, 'Have you seen the notice?' It just said in big letters, 'Guard Dogs On Patrol'.

We started scurrying our way back to the fence but as we did a car drove up towards us, so we legged it and slid under this Winnebago that was parked up nearby. We lay there waiting for the car to go away, and when it eventually did we jumped over the fence and ran back to the bus. On the way I'd stubbed my toe on a grate. That really hurt! Just as we got inside we heard this massive barking from right outside. It sounded like the Hound of the Baskervilles! We didn't jump over the fence again – we stuck to playing Fifa!

Harry: We should probably point out that we don't just mess about! Far from it, tour rehearsals can be really hard work. Rewarding, though. We tend to arrive at rehearsals about 12-ish, having sometimes been in a writing session the night before. We grab something to eat from catering, then head over to the back of the stage to start rehearsals. Right at the start, we're taken through each song by our musical director, so we know where and when all our respective parts kick in. In this case, the sheer size of the stage took some getting used to – it takes a while just to walk to the far end!

Niall: Typically we'll rehearse till about 3.30 or 4, then have a little break before starting again and working till early evening. Then we either head off home, hang out in the tour buses or sometimes dive into a London studio for writing sessions.

Liam: It's during rehearsals and then on tour that the relationships within the band are at their best. Our friendships have inevitably changed since we first got together. Being around each other so much can be quite intense, but we seem to have developed a really good working relationship. We're all good mates, of course, but there are sometimes arguments or differences of opinion that can make things a bit awkward. That's only natural, and it never actually worries any of us, I don't think. You can't spend that much time with a person and not have the odd fall-out. But we always seem to just get on with whatever needs doing. When we're on stage that bond shows the most, because no matter what's happened during the day, once we get on to the stage we're just like, 'YEAH!' There's a love for each other that we have on stage that's paramount to the band. It's where One Direction is at its most exciting. We do spend more time away from each other now, but we're still like brothers. The best brothers ever!

Louis: We started the *Where We Are* world tour just as we were finalising this book, so we have to mention those first few stadium shows in South America. Saying that, it's actually really hard to put into words what it felt like walking out to nearly 40,000 people in Bogotá, Colombia, on our first night! I was so emotional, and it was just the most incredible buzz. We'd worked hard in rehearsals, so to finally get the chance to show our fans what the tour was all about was brilliant.

Liam: Absolutely. We know our band has done well and sold a few records, but standing in front of that many people in these huge venues was just ridiculous. Proper mad. Not exactly the Sunshine Festival, I guess! Seriously, though, how can you describe that? Tens of thousands of people on the other side of the world, crammed into these massive stadiums to see us play. What a privilege. We really upped our game for these concerts. You could see all the lads were just so intent on making these our best shows ever.

Niall: Those shows were just incredible. The noise, the energy from the crowd – the buzz was intense.

Zayn: The fans were rocking up at the hotels and shouting and singing outside. Amazing. The fact we were so far away from home and there were so many fans at these massive gigs was just insane. The shows all have the intensity of that Verona gig I mentioned, only multiplied loads more. It's the best feeling ever.

Harry: Obviously we had to be sensible with our sightseeing this time. We were lucky enough to get to see the Machu Picchu ruins, which were beautiful. Contrast that with playing stadiums, and it really has been an incredible start to the tour. It sums up the band and what our fans have achieved with us. The set list seems to condense all the mad events of the past four years into one night – it's an intense, emotional and amazing experience. I know we've worked really hard and done a good number of gigs, promo, TV, radio, all that. But absolutely nothing beats performing in stadiums around the world … I love it!